PARIS
FOR MEN

PARIS
FOR MEN

THIERRY RICHARD

ILLUSTRATIONS: ASEYN
PHOTOGRAPHY: JULIETTE RANCK

CHÊNE

PLEASE NOTE

As you know time flies, and what some still call "progress" affects us all. Therefore the addresses in this guidebook may well change, though they were correctly listed at the time of going to press. As we've mostly selected establishments of high quality and tradition, it is highly unlikely that there are plenty of errors. However it would be wise to exercise caution by calling ahead, and on exceptional occasions, you may have to be a little indulgent.

THE ART
OF ESCAPE

Paris doesn't exist. We all have our own sort of sentimental geography, our own memory of a Paris enjoyed day by day and dreamt about by night: there are as many cities of Paris as there are Parisians. And since we live here in this unique place, we all share our own view of its different places, moods, enthusiasms, and charms. For a change of perspective, all we have to do is take a little sidestep to find new sources of interest in its well-trodden streets. It's this sidestep I encourage you to take in following me.

These pages are a condensed version of the Paris I love. The Paris that offers infinite sources of pleasure to the men who take the trouble to get to know it. Reread the memoires of Giacomo Casanova: "Cultivating my sensual pleasures was the main business of my entire life; I never had a more important one. Feeling I was born for the opposite sex, I have always loved it, and I saw to it that I was loved as much as possible. I was also transported by my love for a good meal, and I was passionate about every object made to arouse curiosity." It isn't so much a philosophy – or bit of one – as the storyline of this work. Perhaps of my life.

Yet we know all too well that the times never play along with us. The opposing winds of consumption, too much information, and too many distractions and obligations are constantly blowing. But there is no reason we must follow time's rules. After all, we can rather easily make a detour, take the road less travelled. Quietly slip down a divergent path and escape. Enjoy a manly moment even in the most innocent of pleasures, i.e. muse over a cup of morning espresso at the counter, contemplate women's legs from the vantage point of a café terrace, run off to the cinema on a weekday, decide to wear a wool tie, change your cologne when the season changes, or stop and gaze at the clouds hovering over the Jardin des Tuileries.

Do you need a guidebook? No. What you need, rather, is a trip. Tour Paris for the pleasures it offers men. Approach it through the hedonism of the street, check out the special charms that make life happy for Parisian men. Even if these charms must be smuggled. This isn't a catalogue, a phone book, an inventory of "must-dos or die" of Paris addresses. I just wanted to share my pleasures along with the shops, restaurants and places that house them.

So that's it. My Paris is here, in the pages that follow. And this Paris of men's pleasures is also yours.

THIERRY RICHARD

MAI   81

"I know this city by heart; I could take it down stone by stone and rebuild it somewhere else. I've seen it in various aspects: changing Paris, four-seasons Paris, twelve-months-of-the-year Paris, everyday Paris. I've seen it white with snow, blue, clear with frost; I've seen it poor, abandoned, inhabited, in the dark; I've seen it rich and decorated with flags. I've seen it in every way possible. Little by little it's become an old lover, a place so familiar it has no more secrets. I love it. It suits me, I really dig it. And now, we're together for life and death (life for her, death for me)."

HENRI CALET
De ma lucarne

TTLE
NING COFFEE

It's still early. The winter sunshine is finally piercing the clouds, shining on the grey Paris rooftops. The first waves of office workers are pouring out of metro stations onto the streets. You've come out of your half sleep, your bed, your home, but you tell yourself that it's just too early – that you don't really feel ready to plunge into the busyness of the day. So you keep a lookout for the right moment. You're early for your first appointment, after all, or you've dropped the children off at school earlier than usual. Any pretext is good to take a break from obligations. So you've chosen your place carefully, and you open the door. It's a café with just the right amount of patina, an ageless counter, old mirrors, and waiters dressed in black and white. Even heated, the terrace will be for later, when the days will have lengthened and the geraniums are again flowering on balconies. You move away from the counter, wanting to linger a little. You sit alone at a table, not too far from the windows, not too far from the daylight, not too far from the vibe of life outside. You know you're going to plunge back into it, but there's no need to rush. You savour the moment of voluntary exclusion: *"Un café, s'il vous plait."* A tenor voice directly conveys the order: *"Un express!"* You drink the coffee in small sips. The foam is a caramel froth that tickles the lips. It's sweet, a tad acid, and it's bitter, but a swallow of the water you've also ordered will do the trick. You could take out a book or work a little, but this isn't what you want. You want time for yourself, to let your thoughts stray, let them follow your gaze around the room, the morning's regulars, the passersby. Or on the contrary you want to pull yourself into the more distant landscapes of your musings and daydreams. The daily

newspapers are lying around. You pick one up and take your time thumbing through it, yet you don't read everything, either. You take advantage of a few suspended moments, an egotistical pleasure, part inertia, part quietude. You take another sip of coffee but – oops – it's already time. You put your coat back on, not very quickly – why rush – then push through the door. The street noise is the first thing that hits you, ending the break. You pick up your pace as you join the crowd, afraid other people's lives will too soon catch up with your own.

A FEW GOOD SPOTS FOR SAVOURING THE COFFEE:

Au Vieux Colombier
65, rue de Rennes, 6th

A quiet little café with an Art Nouveau decor, not far from the messy busyness of Montparnasse.

Le Rouquet
188, boulevard Saint-Germain, 7th

Just like it was in the 1950s (a real feat for the neighbourhood). You almost expect to come across famous French actors of the times, like Maurice Ronet and Juliette Gréco.

Le Colimaçon
32, rue de Rochechouart, 9th

A mini-café, no bigger than a pocket handkerchief, with four tables only. Straight out of another time and place.

L'Armagnac
104, rue de Charone, 11th

Under a glass and wrought-iron awning, this bistro is all mirrors and woodwork from long ago. The clientele: a ragamuffin and metalworker combo.

More generally, it's an old café that's escaped becoming an orange-and-taupe lounge-bar. Fortunately a few still remain.

FOR REALLY GOOD COFFEE:

Café Verlet
256, rue Saint-Honoré, 1st

This place features colonial flourishes and since 1880 has offered superb grand cru coffee of every origin. Star French chefs Alain Passard, Pierre Gagnaire and Olivier Roellinger come here to stock up. Ask them to make you a Moka-Maragogype (i.e. Ethiopia, Nicaragua), a suave and delightfully aromatic concoction: a real treat.

SECOND-HAND BOOKSELLERS

"One of the pleasures of reading is to discover that a writer who's been dead thirty years can be better than his reputation."
Bernard Frank

The smell of old paper lingers behind the glass door, creaking a bit as it closes, allowing you to slip quietly into this shop decorated in silence.
So many books lie asleep here, you feel like whispering to them. As always, you don't know what you're looking for – in fact, nothing – and that's the charm of venturing into a bookshop. You just push open the door for no reason, for the pleasure of the unexpected: the out-of-print book that you'll carry out like a trophy, by a forgotten writer ushered out by trends and younger writers and now pulled from the annals of history, whom you'll feel you've brought back to life. As yet unknown to you, the book's blurb or beautiful cover will simply win you over. The clerk, quietly seated behind the counter, didn't even look up when you walked in. He's reading.

Your fingers slip over the boxes of books. You skim over the dust jackets, flipping through the books one by one, a parade of old treasures. No, not this one, no... Why not this one? You very carefully dig it out. It's an old book from the 1960 NRF collection, the colour of eggshells. Roger Vailland, *La Fête*. Open it and you breathe in the scent of its dusty pages. The slight smell of ink and nostalgia rise to greet you. The fonts have a long-lost roundness, the pages a velvety thickness that makes you turn them carefully. You read a few lines ("I like a sense of modesty, the absence of a sense of modesty, I don't like immodesty, impudence") and wonder what kind of life it had, what libraries it lived in, whose hands held it, what kind of tears it drew. You're touched to buy a book that has had a life, surviving house moves, successions and disappearances. You like this book already; it has pedigree.

DIG UP OLD BOOKS (AND GIVE THEM AS GIFTS) AT:

Librairie Jousseaume
45-46-47, galerie Vivienne, 2nd – 01 42 96 06 24

Librairie des Archives
83, rue Vieille-du-Temple, 3rd – 01 42 72 13 58

Librairie Ulysse (travel)
26, rue Saint-Louis-en-l'Île, 4th – 01 43 25 17 35

La Rose Noire (erotica)
67, rue Condorcet, 9th – 01 40 16 02 70

Dhouauilly et Cie (children's books)
7, rue de Prague, 12th – 01 43 47 01 20

Apart from the well-known *bouquinistes* along the Seine (Quai du Louvre, Quai de la Tournelle and Quai Voltaire), there are also charming ones in the 9th arrondissement galleries, the Passage Verdeau being my favourite. They also abound in the very literary Latin Quarter (Metro Odéon, toward the Rue de Seine or near the Cour de Rohan).

POLISHING YOUR SHOES

"Don't weigh down your thoughts with the weight of your shoes."
André Breton

Go ahead, you've decided. The time has come. It's a sunny Saturday morning, and the light of Paris is pouring into your apartment. You pull several pair of shoes from the closet where they were snoozing: chukka boots, Oxfords and wingtips. They are all amber coloured, with nuances of brown as light as rosewood or as dark as a drizzle of chocolate. The little wooden shoe kit containing all the polishing tools opens onto a carefully organized mess of metal boxes, brushes, and stiff, smudged rags. The smell of polish hits the nostrils and splashes into the room.

Lined up in orderly fashion, the shoes patiently await their turn. So you gently strip them, removing the cedar shoetree, yanking on the laces until they come out. You do a quick polishing job with the brush and rag. The jar of shoe cream squeaks when you unscrew the top. You plunge the tip of a clean rag – an old shirt – into the cream, and it slides as though into warm butter, bringing back with it a bit of creamy unguent that smells of polish. Then comes the moment you like so much when you rub in the polish with small circular movements. The cream penetrates the skin, effortlessly, as

though along the back of beachgoer on a summer's day. The colour changes a little, veers to mat. The smell of leather becomes stronger; it smells alive, it breathes close by. It's not easy to stop what you're doing and go to the next shoe, repeating the same careful, lustful gestures.

Fortunately, you know you can repeat the ritual the next day. You'll grab the shoes sated with cream, and you'll polish them with wax and water, with the patience of a craftsman and infinitely repeated circular movements. Only then can you imagine the revelation. You'll rub them softly so that they finally shine, these huge puddles of light pouring from our feet. If tomorrow would only come.

READY-TO-WEAR SHOES, OFF THE BEATEN TRACK:

Aubercy
34, rue Vivienne, 2nd
01 42 33 93 61

Discreet, French-style luxury. This bootmaker with a shop in the Bourse area since 1935 blends English quality with Italian creativity and good French taste.
A must-have.
(Starting at €800.)

Hardrige
3, rue Chabanais, 2nd
01 42 96 91 02

A supplier to the elite units of the French army, this Isère-native bootmaker has recently found his place in the ready-to-wear world with affordable customizable models.
(Starting at €250.)

Altan
5, rue Sainte-Beuve, 6th
01 45 44 44 76

This maker of ready-to-wear boots comes from the upper realms of the made-to-measure world, setting himself apart by offering customers completely personalized models (colour, patina, laces, etc). One of the best quality/price ratios on the market.
(Starting at €350.)

Caulaincourt
120, boulevard Haussmann, 8th
01 43 87 03 06

Under the aegis of Alexis Laffont, this young French bootmaker offers contemporary, carefully made Blake-constructed models in quality leather. Limited production, attractive prices.
(Starting at €350.)

Marc Guyot
5, rue Pasquier, 8th
01 47 42 41 84

A really beautiful range of designer shoes of a Roaring Twenties inspiration. Superb patinas to choose from. Really beautiful, original ankle- and workboot models.
(Starting at €500.)

Carlos Santos (at Blake & Goodyear)
46, rue de Longchamp, 16th
01 45 05 14 10

Designed by Marc Guyot, these made-in-Portugal shoes are a blend of elegance and high-quality production. The Handcrafted range is a stylish marvel.
(Starting at €700.)

MORE AFFORDABLE, BUT OF GOOD QUALITY:

Loding
9, rue de Passy, 16th
01 45 20 95 59
(Starting at €150.)

BOOTMAKERS SPECIALISING IN LUXURY MADE-TO-MEASURE BOOTS:

Pierre Corthay
1, rue Volney, 2nd
01 42 61 08 89

Clairvoy
17, rue Fontaine, 9th
01 48 74 44 03

Anthony Delos
41, rue Volta, 3rd
contact@anthonydelos.com
(by appointment only)

(Count on spending no less than €2,500.)

SHOEMAKERS:

Minuit moins 7
10, passage Véro-Dodat, 1st
01 42 21 15 47

Dominique Barilero
5, rue Amélie, 7th
01 45 51 29 53

Hamil
111, rue du Faubourg-Poissonnière, 9th
01 42 46 88 45

Oum Sack
64, rue Blomet, 15th
01 45 66 44 76

Rachid
72, rue Boursault, 17th
01 42 28 00 04

Atelier Cattelan
2, rue Melingue, 19th
01 42 08 58 18

KEEPING THE BEAUTIES BEAUTIFUL

Polishing shoes is a necessary art. Keeping our beautiful shoes beautiful for a long time requires regular, methodical care and attention. The first platitude we have to shelve is that polishing only serves to make shoes shiny. As such, polishing isn't for maintenance; it doesn't nourish the leather. Below is how to go about it so your shoes stay impeccable for years, sometimes for life.

Cleanse your shoes of impurities with a cloth and soft brush. Using a cotton rag, rub a cream suited to the entire surface of the leather (only one brand possible: Saphir). Leave on for 24 hours. Place the shoetrees into the shoes. Still using the cotton rag, mix a little of the polish with water (a drop into the cover of the box) and rub it in, in concentric circles. This step is called "glazing." Let dry for one hour. Then blow on the shoe to create a kind of fog, and rub lightly with a pair of women's pantyhose rolled into a ball, until your shoes shine "like a mirror in a bordello," according to the expression coined at John Lobb.

LEGS AKIMBO

*"Any true gaze
is a desire."*
Alfred de Musset

In 1977, François Truffaut had Charles Denner say these definitive words: "Women's legs are compasses, striding the world in every direction, giving it balance and harmony." This was in Truffaut's film The Man Who Loved Women. A few of us have tattooed this maxim into our being. We've made it a mainstay of life. Our eyes filled with wonder, we've savoured the truth of it in all its exactness on the return of spring every year.

It has to be said that the return of spring is a blessed time for thrill seekers. The light ushers in a triumphal return, shining over the city in a vast white puddle, skimming the ground when evening comes, outlining shapely, scintillating figures. The heat rises along your neck like the fragrance of violet, undressing women as they stand before their closets in the morning.

Out with coats, pants, heavy fabrics. In with lightness. In these times, napes of necks appear, shoulders and arms are bared, legs are revealed, with or without a last rampart of silk: knees and ankles offer themselves up to the sun and men's eyes.

But, do we really have to be stupid to be carried away by the sight of a calf, stretched like the bow of a violin because of a high heel? Do we have to be sickly sentimental to be so moved by a bared thigh, by skin we imagine to be as soft, as hot as the fine sand of the wildest beaches? Aren't we infinitely foolish for smiling blissfully in a corner as soon as a light skirt, blown by the wind, caresses a beautiful, round, captivating bottom sashaying by? Do we have to be desperately obsessed to let our mind, in the absence of our hands, run up and down these bare legs belonging to unknown women, who are taking over the sidewalks with a decided air? And finally, are we destined to live this much apart from people because we forget ourselves for such long moments in the folds of a skirt lifted up over legs crossed quite high up?

Maybe. Maybe we are all of that – stupid, sentimental, obsessed and terribly foolish. But maybe we are only men. Men who love women.

WHERE TO GO FOR A PLEASANT VIEW
OF THIS LIGHT DANCE OF WOMEN'S LEGS

The Boulevard Saint-Germain remains a must.
The vast theatre of the Avenue Montaigne is great
for watching models from the nearby couture
houses sashaying by. The Place Sainte-Marthe,
like the banks of the Canal Saint-Martin, will
delight those who love flowery and "ethnic" fabrics.
Legs are always tanned around the Jardins du
Ranelagh; skirts well cut in the little alleys of
the Marais. Public parks and gardens offer a quiet
refuge to women students and young mothers.
Not to be underestimated. Finally, for the lucky
(or the most patient): the metro entrance not
far from César's sculpture of the centaur
opposite the Carrefour de la Croix-Rouge. A ditzy
Marilyn type always ends up raising her skirt there.

FRANÇOIS
SIMON

Gourmet food critic

WHAT I ENJOY IN PARIS

You can hold it in a small spoon. It extends from ice cream to ice cream (Grom, rue de Seine, café/yogurt). You enjoy it slowly, extremely slowly. This happy thing is made up of layers, one piled atop the other: you read the newspaper in the sunshine, alone with it, allowing it to disintegrate so its identity as ice cream comes through. If at all possible, this should be the day after an exhausting night and you should be in a semi-coma. Don't speak. Just attach yourself to this little atoll. Like an eye, a round shape, a circle, a children's park. Don't get the small one, go for the maxi. Make it your lunch. Then stagger away through the neighbourhood, humming and taking your time.

CREATING A BOUQUET

"You are the bouquet of your bouquet,
And the flower of its flower, grace and modesty."
Pierre de Ronsard

You should always live among flowers. Every week, buy one from the florist below for the price of a pack of smokes, place it in the middle of a table, on a chimney, and live in its fragrance for a few days. It's such a clearly obvious thing, and yet who thinks about it? Flowers make life more beautiful, fill the days with delicate scents and colours.

Scan the florist's storefront to pick out the basis of a bouquet (roses, peonies, tulips, irises), and let your imagination run. Imagine a canvas. Add a shade to highlight, but no more, then place everything onto a huge bed of deep greenery. Go for restraint, a composition mixing few species. Or, on the contrary, try an explosion of colours, widening the palette of petals and corollas, mixing shapes and shades but never to the point of getting just a hodgepodge. See yourself as painting a moment, where huge stems spring up from your paint, and you daub the flowers with a multicolour brush. You can do a bouquet of country flowers or a minimal, sophisticated composition. Whatever you feel like, whatever the day and destination call for.

You grab a bunch of cut flowers, mixing them with a touch of this and that. You try something then start all over, until you get that indefinable but irrepressible feeling of harmony. You take them to the counter for final assembly, where these loose flowers, like so many notes of music, will get a symphonic touch. Once finished, it seizes you – it's gorgeous. You look at it, smell it, plunging your nose into it. And the beauty of it knocks you out in just one whiff.

Truly, if I were looking for proof of God's existence, I would look first in a flower.

A BEAUTIFUL BOUQUET (FAIL-PROOF) FOR A FEW EUROS:

A small bunch of yellow flowers (roses or tulips depending on the season and arrivals)
A bunch of tiny white flowers (gypsophilia, statice or eupatorium)
A bunch of green chrysanthemums (big pale green balls)
Stems of beargrass (long slim, supple stems without flowers)

Ask to have a round bouquet made for you. Refuse the wrapping paper, only keeping the cellophane.
The clearness of it will bring out your bouquet, its colours alone being enough.

FLORISTS ARE ALSO ARTISTS:

Stéphane Chapelle
29, rue de Richelieu, 1st
01 42 60 65 66

Jardin du Louvre
25, rue du Louvre, 1st
01 42 33 52 72

Odorantes (roses)
9, rue Madame, 6th
01 42 84 03 00

Erick Fabre
52, rue Saint-Dominique, 7th
01 45 55 71 84

Un Jour de fleurs
22, rue Jean-Nicot, 7th
01 45 50 43 54

Le Jardin Saint-Honoré
56, rue du Colisée, 8th
01 42 68 10 96

La Fabrique d'Effets
(organic wine and bouquets of flowers)
104, rue Legendre, 17th
09 62 37 41 02

Luc Deschamps
18, avenue Niel, 17th
01 42 27 98 94

Les Mauvaises Graines (plants only)
25, rue Custine, 18th
01 55 79 71 35

LUXURY FLOWERS:

Lachaume
10, rue Royale, 8th
01 42 60 59 74

René Veyrat
168, boulevard Haussmann, 8th
01 45 62 37 86

A CIGAR BENEATH THE STARS

"The sky is beautiful, it's warm and I feel well."
Guillaume Apollinaire

E verything is a matter of circumstance. But in the end, it's always just about the same story. Dinner is over, you plunge into a comfy happiness, perfectly enhanced by the fragrance of wine. The head feels light, as does the heart. You're alone on the terrace – she has gone back into the hotel room – or you're with some friends who've run aground here. The air is soft and welcoming. Then in walks desire. One last bit of pleasure calls, before going home, before sleep, before forgetting. You could just as well find yourself at a party, in the brouhaha of glasses clinking against decibels. You could have a terrible desire to go onto the balcony for peace and quiet. To escape. This is the moment for a cigar. It's premeditated. You get it out of the case, carry it to the nostrils to sniff its powerful, peppery smell, then press it delicately between the fingers as though to prove its elasticity – thus freshness – and slip it between the lips. You chose one that's not too long (a Robusto), just to tell yourself that you've left for half an hour, no longer.

You light it beneath the stars, protecting the flame in the crook of your hand: Hemingway in the tropics, Mallarmé in Fontainebleau. The first puff, always a bit aggressive, smells like powder. But little by little the rhythm slows, the inhalations are well spaced, the puffs of smoke become milder. You raise your eyes toward the sky, puffing the thick smoke out towards the clouds. The Creole fragrance, of earth and ashes, gently breaks up into the air, without bothering anyone at all. Sometimes the desire to walk comes over you and you take a few steps, the tobacco roll glowing in hand, the mind wandering. You take another puff, and continue down to the last one, when the tip is so close it burns your fingers, like a little bit of domestic hell being consumed between your lips. So you crush the tip between two fingers, conscientiously. And toss the body into the lawn or the first flowerpot you see. Even more casual. Nonchalant.
Conscience diluted in the haze of smoke.

CIGARS WITHOUT THE HANG-UPS

SIX IDEAS FOR A SUCCESSFUL FIRST TASTE:

1 Be ready. If you feel stressed out or too tired, cancel the idea, get out of it, put it off till later. A forced or hesitant tasting will leave a bad memory. This isn't what you want, right?

2 Be alone or with the right person. There is nothing like smoking a cigar with good friends, or all by your lonesome self. Cigars are a welcoming parenthesis, their comfort pampering. Among friends tongues become untied, and confidences are shared. Alone, you easily slip off into a realm of reverie. In any case, avoid those who would give lessons.

3 Alert your senses, except your hearing. Take the cigar, feel its velvety softness, breathe in its fragrance, admire its construction, snip off the tip and put it in your mouth. Rolling it between the fingers near your eardrum will give you no indication of its quality. Leave that to mafia types and cowboys.

4 Forget the little number about cigar etiquette. Only false prophets affirm that cigar smoking is some kind of ceremony. Remove the paper ring at the beginning or at the end, as you feel, then hack off the tip guillotine style, cleanly and sharply, with the nails or teeth. Then puff away as you like. There are only two rules to follow: never carry a flame along its fragile skin, and don't light it with lighter fluid, as this may change how it tastes. And of course, don't swallow its smoke.

5 Leave your head in the cloakroom. Woody? Roasted? The taste of leather, wild game, spices, honey? So what. What if you simply let your pleasures take over? Avoid too much intensive studying. Mysteries are not to be explained. It's just as well not to decipher this first sensual moment. You'll be academic the next times.

6 Don't hesitate to say goodbye to it. Even at half the cigar, if you think it has said everything to you (and vice versa), if you feel a slight light-headedness take over, put an end to the union. Forcing yourself to finish is absolutely not a must. Stop the moment the pleasure threatens to abandon you.

FIND YOUR FAVORITES:

La Civette
du Palais-Royal
157, rue Saint-Honoré, 1st
01 42 96 04 99

The oldest cigar shop in France, opened in 1717 opposite the Comédie-Française. Voltaire, Casanova and Napoleon III purchased their cigars here.

Art Tabac
2, place de Catalogne, 14th
01 40 47 66 50

The owner of this place is the only one in France to have created his own cigar, the Pitbull, in Nicaragua. Excellent selection of Havanas and other cigars. Features a smoking room.

AND ALSO:

Civette George V
22, avenue George-V, 8th
01 47 23 44 75

Le Lotus
4, rue de l'Arcade, 8th
01 42 65 35 36

Lemaire
59, avenue Victor-Hugo, 16th
01 45 00 75 63

ALONE
AMONG WOMEN

"All these women sitting here have something very pleasant at heart: a memory, an expectation."
Jules Renard

You know it as soon as you open the door. A brief look at the menu confirms it. Salads, savoury pies, sprouts, wheat germ and strange grains and fruit cereals (how that carrot-orange-ginger juice concoction at Nanashi excites you), dozens of British-style pastries (the cheese cake is a must): you are entering unknown territory. Because here, as you can see, skirts reign supreme. You are among women, in one of these places dubbed "girls only."

Of course, you've only come for lunch, and preferably alone. Long legs slide beneath the tables, handbags are asleep next to the feet of chairs like docile pets. The subtle fragrance of well-brushed hair weaves through the tables. Entire concerts of kisses ring out with arrivals, and high voices blend with the whispers of the unfaithful. Confidences and rumours are on the menu. You are the man lost among women, and they have the natural elegance not to let you feel it.

So mixed with the pleasure of nice little dietetically correct dishes – one time doesn't make it a habit, and frankly it's reinvigorating – is the thrill of sliding your eyes from table to table, like a long take in a film by Claude Lelouch, their favourite filmmaker. In a decor that's always elegant and pretty with feminine touches, as perfect as the last manicure, the mind wanders with each mouthful. All kinds of women are within reach of the imagination, in keeping with the atmosphere and locale: sophisticated, spiritual, futile, absent-minded, outrageous, regressive, chirpy (sometimes it's the aviary), detached, charming, concentrated, fashionable. There are even young mothers in their beautiful prime and full of adventure.

You'll keep your thoughts to yourself but will come out with the stomach and the heart feeling light, delighted to have dared to slip into their lair, happy because of all that grace but a bit melancholic, even so. You were only passing. A guest in transit. A man alone among the women.

WHERE TO GO?
(One at a time, please, sirs.)

Cantine de Merci
111, boulevard Beaumarchais, 3rd
01 42 77 00 33

Cru
7, rue Charlemagne, 4th
01 40 27 81 84

Les Deux Abeilles
189, rue de l'Université, 7th
01 45 55 64 04

Rose Bakery
46, Rue des Martyrs, 9th
01 42 82 12 80

Supernature
12, rue de Trévise, 9th
01 47 70 21 03

Nanashi
31, rue de Paradis, 10th
01 40 22 05 55

And all the Bon Marché restaurants
24, rue de Sèvres, 7th
01 42 22 81 60

WHAT ABOUT TEATIME?

Carette
25, place des Vosges, 3rd
01 48 87 94 07

Salon du cinéma du Panthéon
13, rue Victor Cousin, 5th
01 56 24 88 80

Ladurée
21, rue Bonaparte, 6th
01 44 07 64 87

Bread and Roses
7, rue de Fleurus, 6th
01 42 22 06 06

Café du Musée Jacquemart André
158, boulevard Haussmann, 8th
01 45 62 11 59

THE CITY AT DUSK

*"You have to capture the light
and throw it directly onto the canvas."*
Claude Monet

Without a doubt this always been the hour I take the greatest pleasure in savouring. Always? Let's say, ever since that long-ago time when as children, we took long trips in the car from Paris to the Riviera. I would tune out the radio my parents listened to and find myself, forehead stuck to the window, absorbed in watching the clouds at nightfall. The reflections of metallic light, glowing and so special, fascinated me.

Paris at dusk is the between-times moment; it's instability par excellence, when things dissolve. It's not yet night-time but not really daytime. The sky is tinted with every possible variation of blue, violent and dark in some places, lit with milky paleness in others. The outline of the city becomes more exact, sharpened by the last rays of the sun, dying in orange. People wrap themselves up in this passing, moving light with golden reflections. You stop. You look. Everything seems so different from what it was a few moments before, and from what it will be in a few more minutes, when the night will finally become mistress of the place, under the moon, the stars or the streetlamps.

Everything is suspended. A minute more, and it's the last loop, the ultimate flash of chiaroscuro revealing the city's hidden beauties; as though the real nature of Paris abruptly emerged, for hardly a few seconds, before disappearing into the shadows. Perspectives become erased, slowly sliding into pastel softness. That's when everything seems possible.

WHAT TO VIEW AT THE END OF THE DAY

The Pont Alexandre-III and the Pont des Arts
The tip of Ile Saint-Louis
The edges of the Bois de Boulogne
The riverbank in front of the Musée d'Orsay
The gates of the Parc du Buttes-Chaumont
Place de Breteuil, looking towards the dome of Les Invalides
The straight alleys of the Jardins du Palais-Royal
The rooftop of the Opéra
Everywhere else

WEARING A TIE

"A cravat worn well influences the entire dress, like an exquisite perfume; it is to the outfit what the truffle is to the dinner."

Honoré de Balzac

The times, they are a-changing: what used to be a must is now an option, and as such, a mark of distinction. So it is for the necktie. This vade mecum of the middle manager, essential item of the finance world, has become an element of differentiation, an accident, a rarity. What happy wearers we are. We have the freedom, the choice of situations, the elegance of the moment. The necessary moment is the compensation, chosen with care and discernment (when to wear it, when not to). We display our necktie like an old mistress, on whim, sometimes serious and grave, other times full of imagination.

There you are, your body bent over the drawer in which they lie side-by-side, or carefully rolled into multicolour snails as you caress the fabrics and colours with a hungry eye. Your fingers slide, grazing the silk, lightly touching the wool, rubbing the knits. The circumstances are variable. You can go out to dinner with her, run to the opera or the theatre, or you could also, in a back room, prepare to join several friends or family members to uncork a few bottles.

The time to pick one has come. Every detail has its significance: the material (the suppleness of a jacket or poplin calls for a light tie); the tone (the match with the shirt or jacket should look like an obvious choice); and the size of the knot (bigger on an Italian collar and tighter on an English one). A few minutes go by as you try a few colours and materials, as you think a little. Finally you sling your selection around your raised collar.

The final moment of sensual pleasure comes: it is tucked away in the precise

Always wear a tie in Paris to:
- go to a performance (no, not the cinema),
- be interviewed on television,
- have dinner in a top restaurant to annoy the bobos.

WHERE TO GO FOR TO FIND THE BEST ONES:

Charvet
28, place Vendôme, 1st
01 42 60 30 70

Brooks Brothers
372, rue Saint-Honoré, 1st
01 40 20 10 01

Hackett
17, rue de Sèvres, 6th - 01 45 49 18 93

La Maison de la Cravate
14, rue du Regard, 6th - 01 45 48 66 02

Marinella
(The Rolls Royce of neckties and 9-fold models)
at the Four Seasons George V
31, avenue George V, 8th - 01 49 52 70 00

Kimono
74, boulevard Haussmann, 8th
01 43 87 43 42

Old England
12, boulevard des Capucines, 9th
01 47 42 81 99

A WELL-KEPT SECRET:

Just at the foot of the Printemps Haussmann department store (under the passage leading to Rue de Provence, between Printemps Beauté and Printemps de la Mode), is a stand with French-made neckties where you can get 5 solid ties for €5: enough for you to take yourself for an oil baron!

gestures you've made at least 1,000 times already. Your agile hands slide over the two bits of fabric, then there is the swishing noise when you tighten the knot, the gentle pinching, the Windsor, the half-Windsor, and the final movement that will reveal a the perfect little teardrop beneath the knot. The memory of your father, teaching you how to put it on, emerges, though you haven't exactly called it up. There is the exactness of the length, your liking for various pairings. One last adjustment and you're adorned. You can appear in public, give yourself over nicely to being seen with your tie on. You can wear it with the quiet pride of those who never bend to ordinary rules.

When the 8 o'clock news announcers and politicians no longer wear them, it is time to take them out of the drawer. Because there are no seasons for neckties, just occasions.

FRANCIS KURKDJIAN

Perfumer

GOING HOME BY FOOT

My love for Paris is unconditional. I travel often, and one of my very first pleasures, on return from my professional trips, is to regain possession of my city. I go home by foot from my shop on Rue d'Alger to my home, opposite the Théâtre de la Renaissance in the 10th *arrondissement*: it's a totally Parisian pleasure. I love strolling along Rue Saint-Honoré, stopping a moment before the display window of the Galérie de la Manufacture Nationale de Sèvres on Place André-Malraux, then pass in front of the Comédie-Française thinking of all the plays I won't be able to see due to a lack of time. I like to keep walking under the arcades of the Palais-Royal, slaloming between the children playing in the middle of the Colonnes de Buren, watching the stray tourists walking among them. I like to take the route through the garden, breathe in the smells that change with the seasons, before going back to the noisy street only after this little break outside of time. I like this path that has me sliding imperceptibly from the elegant 1st *arrondissement* toward my adopted neighbourhood, where life is filled with all the savours of the world. I love these familiar colours, smells and noises. I love Paris, its magic and its spirit of freedom.

LIGHTING THE FIRE

"I lived by the sound of crackling flames, by the scent of their warmth."
Paul Eluard

You've put a few newspapers aside and bought kindling wood at a service station on a September weekend. You've hauled a few logs of an appropriate size for Paris into the apartment, measuring them against a 30-cm cord, no more – Haussmann logs.

Lighting a fire is a pleasure you never tire of and one you never hand over to someone else. It's an old reflex, a rural one that's been with us since the dawn of time; and it's a guy's job. Your pride in it is a little boy's. And everyone has their own technique, perfected whenever possible (scout camp, summer barbecues, weekends in the country). Any occasion is good. It's the result that counts, a fire that spits crackling flames to the top of the hearth, bathed in orange light.

First you crinkle the newspapers into loose balls, with the inconsequential delight of getting ink all over your fingers. Then you scatter the little bits of kindling,

WHERE TO GO TO BUY WOOD
IN PARIS

To neighbourhood service
stations, or what is left of them,
and into DIY or gardening
chain stores. One efficient,
quick solution is to have home
deliveries made:
(www.bucheabuche.fr and
www.lebucheronparisien.com).

DINING BY FIRELIGHT:

La Chinoiserie
24, boulevard Malesherbes, 8th
01 55 27 12 34

Chic, contemporary, ideal
for lovers out dining (request
one of the two tables near
the chimney).

L'Atelier de Maître Albert
1, rue Maître-Albert, 5th
01 56 81 30 01

Contemporary rotisserie and
Middle-Ages fireplace, under
the aegis of Guy Savoy.

Le Chalet des Îles
Lac Inférieur, bois de Boulogne, 16th
01 42 88 04 69

Worth it especially for
the setting, a superb room
with a fireplace, once
frequented by Proust.

whose woodsy smell is like an appetizer. You like
sniffing the fibrous smell, scooping the wood bits
up in handfuls just to hold them to your nose like
fragrant flowers. You scatter some of them with
slow, calculated movements, creating a star shape
on top of the small, newly created pile. Now comes
the tricky moment of actually lighting the fire using
the matches as long as cathedral candles. You hold
the lit match out to the right, toward the middle, to
the left; the paper curls back with a crinkling sound,
creating sudden tall, heatless flames. You watch
how the kindling is taken up in flames, the mix of
red and black, how the wood suddenly palpitates
with life, when only seconds before it was inanimate.

The reward is there in the sputtering of flames,
in the orange and blue heat dancing over the faces
of those around, in the crackling of wood; the
bellows will be for later. Winter can come now.
You're ready for it.

JOGGING
IN PARIS
WITHOUT COMING
ACROSS A CAR

It is possible to go for a jog in Paris without seeing any car at all (or hardly a car), while savouring the soul of the city along the Seine. You just have to follow the itinerary below (about 10 km):

1. Start on the North side of the Jardins du Palais-Royal, in front of the Grand Véfour restaurant;

2. Jog through the gardens, under the arcades, and cross the courtyard by the Colonnes de Buren;

3. Come out on the Place Colette, between the Comédie-Française and Le Nemours café;

4. Head along the Place du Palais-Royal toward the Louvre;

5. Cross Rue de Rivoli and go under the Louvre's arches until you get to the Pyramid;

6. Turn right to cross the Carrousel roundabout, then jog through the small Arc de Triomphe du Carrousel erected by Napoleon;

7. Continue straight on for about ten paces, so that you can enter the Jardin des Tuileries;

8. Do a tour of gardens. Or rather three-fourths of them, because on its south flank, a tunnel leads to the Simone-de-Beauvoir footbridge and the pedestrian banks of the Seine near the barges;

9. Stay on the Right Bank and continue on the banks toward the Eiffel Tower;

10. Keep going for a few hundred meters: the path starts to climb until you reach the obelisk at Place de la Concorde, before going down again to water level;

11. Further along on the banks, turn around before you get to the influx of tourist buses around the Bateaux Mouches or (if you have the courage) change banks at Pont de l'Alma and continue on to the Champ-de-Mars;

12. Turn around and head back the same way you came.

At the end of your run, when you reach the iron gate in front of the Grand Véfour, take the time to enjoy the water fountain and chairs awaiting you in the garden, after doing a few stretches under the trees. Your muscles are in pain, your soul is quiet, and your eyes are full of the sites you have seen: the Grand Palais, the Eiffel Tower, the Louvre, the Musée d'Orsay, the bridges. You'll realize your heart was beating in the heart of Paris.

YOU DON'T NEED TO RUN MARATHONS TO GET WHAT YOU NEED:

Boutique du Marathon
26, rue Léon-Jost, 17th – 01 42 27 48 18

Planet Jogging
58, avenue de la Grande-Armée, 17th – 01 45 72 40 00

Endurance Shop
14, rue de l'Ouest, 14th – 01 43 27 15 65

Opened by jogging enthusiasts, these shops offer the special feature of testing your running style on video, on a conveyer belt, to recommend the shoes that are best adapted to your morphology. They also offer some people the chance to try shoes on the street, in any kind of weather.

JOGGING IN PARIS
WITHOUT COMING ACROSS A CAR

TIME FOR DINNER

"You see that reinforcements are arriving,
we need more victuals."
Alexandre Dumas

Men keep up their friendships through rituals. So in Paris, at the first sign of a cold snap in autumn, pullovers come out of the closet as the biting chill of evening falls earlier and earlier and strange gatherings occur at the bistros abandoned all summer. It's September again, when men dine together.

They gather in old restaurants with a faux 19th-century, Third-Republic air, savouring time's passage over dishes as solid as the appetites they brag about. On such evenings it's goodbye to steamed sea bass with fennel and scallops *a la plancha*. Those are for dining lovers. Now's the time for pork of every kind. The offal glows in the plate, the cheese is strong, the wine straightforward. Back again are 19th-century tastes, terrines and game, men in shirtsleeves, and lots of wine. There are never fewer than three guys at the table, and rarely are there as many as six: they have to hear one another. In the warmth of emptied glasses

and the comfort of a timeless decor, the thermostat of human relations runs high. Banalities are done with quickly, professional ups and downs are discussed, news about the youngest child is given. The men are in France, so they talk about food. It's a habit they've never shaken: the latest restaurant discovery, the wine they got from the wine cellar, how their meal tastes. A few

more mouthfuls, and the subject turns to politics, as always. Sometimes the exchanges are heated, and voices rise as high as the soufflé au Grand Marnier. No harm is ever done, however, as they know each other so well. Finally they detour into cultural matters: they love books and movies. And women, of course.

Now it all comes out, they slowly spill their secrets, things they never tell their companions. It's the reeling out of unedited soul-searching. Here nothing is taboo; friends bare their feelings with no discomfort.

Then they'll each go their separate ways, a bit gray, a bit pink, still wrapped in the warmth of the moment they spent together. They are happy to have spent it. This season will last till spring, when their gatherings will become more and more spaced out as the days lengthen. Then summer will come, and they will scatter to the four corners of the earth, filling up the tank for future conversations.

Which will take place as soon as they get back to Paris.

TO REMAKE THE WORLD OVER A PLATE OF LENTILS, HEAD TO:

Le Pantruche

3, rue Victor-Massé, 9th
01 48 78 55 60

Having trained with Éric Fréchon, who was awarded 3 Michelin stars at the restaurant Epicure in the hotel Le Bristol, Franck Baranger delivers top flight cuisine in his neighbourhood bistro, at indulgent prices.
One dish: braised beef cheeks in red wine sauce, carrots with black pepper.
One price: €32 for the menu.

Glou

101, rue Vieille-du-Temple, 3rd
01 42 74 44 32

In a New York loft décor, light-hearted diners sit at big communal tables to nibble well-chosen foods that they wash down with very clever wines.
One dish: penne with squid ink and *poutargue*.
One price: between €30 and €50.

Chez Grenouille

52, rue Blanche, 9th
01 42 81 34 07

For those who have no fear of calories (the house *andouillette* is one for the books), Grenouille shows talent reviving country cuisine: it's generous and without hang-ups.
One dish: andouillette with foie gras and escargots.
One price: between €40 and €50.

Laiterie Sainte-Clotilde

64, rue de Bellechasse, 7th
01 45 51 74 61

This restaurant, a prototype for dining with friends, will make you feel you're one of the family after the second visit. The welcome is unbeatably kind, the plates of food pretty.
One dish: pork filet mignon with sage and rhubarb.
One price: between €25 and €40.

L'Ami Jean

27, rue Malar, 7th
01 47 05 86 89

The highly charged atmosphere of this old restaurant (and the vociferous activity of its chef, Stéphane Jégo) adds to the frenzy of the wonderfully imaginative, hearty dishes.
One dish: Wagyu beef and cepes.
One price: €35 for the menu.

Le J'Go

4, rue Drouot, 9th
01 40 22 09 09

Going to the Stade de France on a rugby night is a must for guys in Paris, who have not forgotten what their town owes to Southwest France, though deprived of its stadiums.
One dish: skewered farm-raised leg of Quercy lamb and Tarbe white beans.
One price: between €30 and €40.

Septime

80, rue de Charonne, 11th
01 43 67 38 29

Very straightforward, fresh dishes by a young chef formerly with Alain Passard (who was awarded 3 Michelin stars at his restaurant L'Arpège).
Beautiful, uncluttered decor of stone and dark wood, in tune with the times.
One dish: *gnochetti* with sweet grits and aged Mimolette cheese shavings.
One price: €26 (fixed-price menu).

L'Escarbille

8, rue de Vélizy, Meudon (92)
01 45 34 12 03

The setting is more white tablecloths and silver than rock-and-roll, but the dishes are superb when dinner requires you to wear your necktie.
One dish: Suprême of pigeon *au sang*, pigeon leg confit, and curly kale.
One price: €44 (fixed-price menu).

AND OF COURSE, TO THE BEST GOURMET BISTROS:

Comptoir du Relais
9, carrefour de l'Odéon, 6th
01 44 27 07 97

Bistrot Paul Bert
18, rue Paul-Bert, 11th
01 43 72 24 01

Le Baratin
3, rue Jouye-Rouve, 20th
01 43 49 39 70

GOING TO THE MOVIES ON A WEEKDAY AFTERNOON

"Of all the schools I went to, the best was the school of life, and it's the one I benefited from the most."
Anatole France

Give yourself a break, hurry up and slow down. Allow yourself a little time to leave the present for two hours straight. Go to the movies in mid-afternoon, on a workday.

The excitement starts when you're in the queue. It's never very long on a Tuesday at 3pm: there are a few students, a few people of a mature age, a few dilettantes; the crowd is not big and booming crowds like on weekends.

And in fact you speak softly to buy your ticket, as though you don't want anyone to notice you for the venial sin you are committing.

In general, in exceptional circumstances, you avoid major feature films. Of course you want to escape, but subtly, without fanfare. And this begins as soon as you enter the room, way too big for the small group carefully placed around it. Silent and welcoming in the soft chiaroscuro, its seats call out to you like the psychoanalyst's sofa. You sink comfortably into one, with your cap and coat to the left, backpack to the right, stretching your legs out diagonally. Sometimes in the smaller cinemas, for a film that's for a small audience, there will only be a handful of viewers, three or four at the very most. Then you feel you are at home in your own giant room. Yet this feeling is mixed with the

weird feeling of being something of an outsider, an infringement, where you steal a moment to relax from some other indefinable person. The little tweak to your conscience adds to the shameful, furtive, stolen pleasure.

You sink into silence, rocked by the irregular murmuring of the other spectators. It's the decompression chamber, the rite of passage that snatches you from the reality of the world and quietly leads you to where the lights are off. The screen becomes alive under the projector lights. We straighten ourselves a little, as at takeoff. Then we're off. The trip can begin. And so can the dream.

Two hours later, on the sidewalk, you're finished playing hooky. You join the ranks, your head still elsewhere. You slightly regret not having asked the young woman sitting next to you to go and have a coffee to talk about Sautet and Antonioni. Another time, maybe.

Meanwhile, it has started to rain.

CINEMAS WITH A CHARM BEYOND THEIR SCREENS:

Le Champo
51, rue des Écoles, 5th
01 43 54 51 60

Le Saint-Germain-des-Prés
22, rue Guillaume-Apollinaire, 6th
01 42 22 87 23

Le Nouvel Odéon
6, rue de l'École-de-Médecine, 6th
01 43 26 19 68

La Pagode
57, rue de Babylone, 7th
09 62 23 05 33

Le Balzac
1, rue Balzac, 8th
01 45 61 10 60

Le Cinéma des Cinéastes
7, avenue de Clichy, 17th
08 92 68 97 17

Le Mac-Mahon
5, avenue Mac-Mahon, 17th
01 43 80 24 81

Le Studio 28
10, rue Tholozé, 18th
01 46 06 36 07

FRÉDÉRIC
BEIGBEDER

Writer, Film-maker

Want to share a pleasure?
Two scrambled eggs with truffles at the Maison de la Truffe, place de la Madeleine.

A pleasure of childhood?
Shrimp fishing on Cenitz beach at Guéthary.

A scented pleasure?
The kitchen smell of my grandmother's applesauce, in Pau.

Pleasure for the ears?
Frédéric Chopin.

A carnal pleasure?
Do you want phone numbers?

A pleasure to the tastebuds?
Cheese, preferably a Vacherin from Barthélémy in December.

A very expensive pleasure?
The Falcon 900 for a flight to Venice (€40,000) to have a carpaccio at Harry's Bar.

An anachronistic pleasure?
Reading.

An unknown pleasure?
I've never jumped with a parachute.

A pleasure that costs nothing?
Crossing the Pont des Arts at dusk.

A shameful pleasure?
Signing autographs in Cannes.

An illegal pleasure?
Sniffing a line of coke on the hood of a car.

An overestimated pleasure?
Same as above.

A typically Parisian pleasure?
The Square du Vert-Galant, undoubtedly the most beautiful spot in Paris, in the middle of the Seine. It's like an unmoving steamship. In spring, take a young girl in full flower there before throwing yourself off the Pont Neuf, to drown yourself beneath a Bateau-Mouche.

THE EROTIC POTENTIAL OF SAYING "VOUS"

"Sensual delight likes a sense of modesty."
Philippe Sollers

We've been pleasantly chatting for scarcely hour in the shadowy light of the Mezzanine de la Rive Gauche. I haven't taken my eyes off her. I like how the little blond, clear bangs fall against the beautiful curve of her neck beneath her chignon; the way she crosses her legs very high, with a good slant, as though an accident might well occur; I like how her clear laughter rebels against her gravelly voice. Her eyes hold haughty, provocative fires. The subtle game of seduction has begun, move for move, until the final checkmate.

She slowly raises her coupe to her lips, takes a sip of champagne and rests it on the coffee table with captivating aristocratic nonchalance. Silence. With one last, cheeky look she finally comes out with the highly dreaded remark: "We should say 'tu' to each other, don't you think?"

I close my eyes and mouth with a sigh. *Non, non, non!* Why do people always want to take short cuts, dashing through fields and skipping the steps? Saying "vous" is great! It creates this pleasant distance between people that materializes the effort of making a conquest. You have all these charming obstacles to overcome, the Wolf's jump of feelings to get past, all these sweet barricades to knock down. It's always really sensual to use "vous," which you keep using even as you get to know more about the other person, as you gain a fuller knowledge of them. There's a sort of respect, a high form of refinement perhaps. It's definitely a game.

Continuing to use "vous" is also saving the pleasure of a wonderful moment to come, when you'll slip over to using "tu," as though you are abandoning something, mutually turning in your weapons. When the hands touch or the bodies burn with desire. This pure, ephemeral moment where the intimacy crystallizes around one word only. "Tu."

So why deprive yourself?

HAVING
A COCKTAIL
MADE FOR YOU

"When the soul is thirsty, it must quench its thirst."
Victor Hugo

Really, we should always thank bartenders, slip them a bill when we leave, like we do with a shrink.

They are ever present behind the bar, like a stopover, the last wall of civilization. Whether they work in the pettily luxurious atmosphere of palace hotel, are on cosy terms with Hemingway, or are ordinary pickpockets, they are always there on difficult days. They see you come along tired, stressed out, excited, in love, sometimes even absent. They see you alone or with friends. You offer yourself up to their judgment, tell them your worries, and tell them what you desire right now: "Something a little spicy, a bit acid, without much fruit but refreshing." Their eyes sparkle, they start to see more clearly. They outline the shapes, tune up their violins: "What about starting with a little touch of mescal, would that do? You don't dare tell him you don't know what mescal is, that you trust him and he must know what he's doing. Because actually the most important thing is what you don't say: that a young woman has been following you around, like your very soul, for the past few days. You with your three-day beard, your rumpled jacket. All of that goes into the shaker. With three grape seeds and a hint of ginger ale. You watch him make the drink. His eyes are lost in his precise movements and the incessant spurts of liquid. The sound of ice cubes being crushed is a shock to the soft salsa background music. It makes its way through the bursts of cosmopolitan voices. Then everything stops. It's like slow motion as the drink comes out all golden and clinking. There is a final squeeze of lime. He smiles at you as you start to sip it.

Wow! All your moods are right there, the mood of the moment and the moments to come. It's a mixture of flavours and smells; an uppercut, an embrace, a whisper in the ear. At the bottom of the glass, there is life.

BARTENDERS BEHIND OLD BARS:

Bar Hemingway (hôtel Ritz)
15, place Vendôme, 1st – 01 43 16 33 65

Duke's Bar (hôtel Westminster)
13, rue de la Paix, 2nd – 01 42 61 55 11

MODERN BARS:

Le Wildrick's
95, rue Saint-Honoré, 1st – 01 40 28 02 62

Experimental Cocktail Club
37, rue Saint-Sauveur, 2nd – 01 45 08 88 09

Le Molotov
4, rue de Port-Mahon, 2nd – 01 73 70 98 46

Curio Parlor
16, rue des Bernardins, 5th
01 44 07 12 47

Prescription Cocktail Club
23, rue Mazarine, 6th – 01 46 34 67 73

Le Secret
16, avenue de Friedland, 8th
01 53 53 02 02

MY HIDEOUT:

La Candelaria
52, rue de Saintonge, 3rd – 01 42 74 41 28

This place has a clandestine, South American feel. It's hidden in the back of a *taquería*, where my favourite bartenders work: the Colombian Carina and the New Yorker Joshua.

DRIVING
AN OLD CAR

*"Cars were my dancers . . . During long nights of travel,
I would stop on lesser used roads to sleep in them,
like an exhausted lover, my cheek pressed against
their leather cushions."*
Michel Déon

Not all cars are automobiles. Far from it. They are stuck being useful and the luggage in their XXL trunks hold no emotion. Other cars, however, are spellbinding and pretentious. They're the ones we like. They're the Holy Graal of the mechanical world: real automobiles. "Need a lift? Sounds good, doesn't it? Too old? Too old-school? Oh, well. What do you care? You like driving a vintage car in the streets of Paris. Weaving down the boulevards at the wheel of one, affirming your taste for independence and adventure, in fact your taste, period. Driving a vintage automobile, as you know, is something.

Of course, there is the beauty of the engine. Its old-fashioned lines, when every car still had its own personality and didn't try to look like the trendiest thing on the road, or to have universally round, safe shapes, like a protective cocoon or your mother's tummy. Men fashioned heavy materials like stainless steel, chrome and rubber into a desirable object.

A vintage car carries an entire era with it, as though all the years past had found refuge in its glove compartment. Slide into a Lotus Seven and the 1960s tumble out in force, Swinging London, Mary Quant, miniskirts and all. Climb into a Porsche 911 Targa and all of the sudden, before your eyes are

ALL RIGHT, LET'S GO! *

OUR FAVOURITE DEALERSHIP:

Christophe Pund
La Galerie des Damiers, Mont des Récollets,
59670 Cassel - 03 28 40 59 24

AND ALSO:

L'Atelier 46
9, rue Paul-Napoléon Roinard, 92400 Courbevoie
01 56 05 46 46

Mécaniques Modernes et Classiques
136, boulevard Suchet, 16th - 01 46 47 29 29

Avanti Motors
15, avenue Rapp, 7th - 01 44 18 95 00

**NOT TO MENTION, OF COURSE,
THE AUCTION HOUSES**

Bonhams (Me Jean-Christophe Giuseppi)
4, rue de la Paix, 1st – 01 42 61 10 11

Artcurial (département Automobile)
7, rond-point des Champs-Élysées, 8th Paris
01 42 99 20 56

Me Jean-Pierre Osenat
5, rue Royale, 77300 Fontainebleau
01 60 72 79 67

Chevau-légers Enchères
(Me Gilles Chausselat)
6 bis, avenue de Sceaux, 78000 Versailles
01 39 50 58 08

* Traditionally, most of these places are located
outside of Paris. Consider this as your first appeal
to burn rubber.

the 1970s: moustaches, Sylvia Kristel
in *Lui* magazine and *Eau Sauvage*. What
can you do? These old crates are time
machines.

And then there's how they smell:
inimitable, shiny, exhilarating.
The smell of petrol rising to the nostrils.
There is nothing antiseptic in them;
just character, sensations. Like when
you drive them, which is more like
piloting. Of course there's that wonderful
cloud hovering over every one of your
outings: the never distant risk of a
breakdown. Name a vintage car lover
who never found himself stranded
on a country road? How many charming
villages would he have totally passed
over, were it not for the mechanical
breakdowns of his vehicle?
The vintage car makes you fatalistic.
And adventuresome.

Driving one in Paris is a true joy, and
an inconvenient one. To treat yourself
to it, you have to stick to one respectable
rule: put style over comfort. A noble plan.

"Being Parisian is neither a function, nor a state, nor a job – yet it's all of that. It's unique and inestimable – and furthermore it's something you can't sell. You are Parisian, or you are not. And those who are not wonder, every morning, what they can do to become one, and these people will never become one. Because being Parisian isn't a question of will or fortune. It's not even a question of values. It's an indefinable blend of spirit, taste, snobbery, happy-go-luckiness, bravura and amorality. In fact you don't have to know why you are Parisian, only why other people are not. A Spaniard can't be a Londoner, an Englishman can't be a Berliner, but an Albanian can be Parisian. Because to be one, you don't have to have been born in Paris or even in France. You need something else. You need to be adopted by all, without anyone talking about it. There's something rather mysterious in these elections, a kind of secret understanding. One is a naturalized Parisian, all of a sudden, one fine evening. Yes, all these people who hate each other, who never leave each other during the year, who share their women, mistresses and friends, who watch each other age but don't see each other change, who make up a real world – I mean a real planet – with its everyday life, recreations, honours, honour and quirks; yes, all these people know how to be in agreement in a moment, when they need to."

SACHA GUITRY
Mémoires d'un tricheur

CHANGING FRAGRANCES EVERY SEASON

"This language will be of the soul for the soul, resuming everything."

Arthur Rimbaud

Really, you don't go by the Gregorian calendar, do you? You don't believe that equinoxes and solstices can't be wrong? That March 20th ushers in springtime? That on September 23rd, the death knell tolls for summer? That the seasons are in line with the calendar? Because they never quite fall on time; sometimes they're late, other times a bit early; you can't rely on dates. When wintry weather persists or a mild, royal blue sky sticks around too long, you have to come up with your own points of reference.

But there is one thing that never fools us. You wake up on a beautiful day, head straight to the shower, pull back the curtains and look at the sky: the present. There are no clouds, the countertops reflect silver light, and down in the street, no one at all is wearing a coat. This morning, it's goodbye to musk, amber, cedar and Russian leather notes. Hello to freshness, bergamot, white flowers and jasmine. The flacons of dark, compelling essences are stored away. Out comes transparency, the clearness of a morning in Greece. You don't quite know why, but for you spring has begun today. The light flowery notes have taken over and will follow you along for these few months of good weather. You feel good. Your soul is serene, wrapped in a fragrance of pure air scented with lemon.

Then a day in October or November will come, when the cold will slip beneath the door, ushering in new desires for the scent of comfort and warmth, a strong, enveloping presence. Your taste for heady scents, for benzoin and incense, will come. You'll want notes of underbrush, notes of the hunt and of evenings at the Opéra to linger. A new season will begin.

FRAGRANT SHOPS FOR A FRAGRANT FEELING:

Jovoy
29, rue Danielle-Casanova, 1st – 01 40 20 06 19

We have a soft spot for this recently opened shop, where the charming, relaxed welcome goes hand in hand with a true concern to teach. Very fine, admirable, smaller, not very well-known brands are sold here (Rancé, L.T. Piver, Isabey, Parfum d'Empire, etc). Workshops initiating you into the world of fragrance are given every Saturday afternoon (€150 per half day).

Marie-Antoinette
place, du Marché-Sainte-Catherine, 4th – 01 42 71 25 07

This shop has that fake look of a red candy shop, but it is charming and discreet, exclusively selling only very beautiful flacons of fragrance (Frapin) and old brands with bewitching scents (Robert Piguet, Lubin, Parfums d'Orsay, among others). There's more than enough to suit your nose here.

AND ALSO:

The Scent Room at Printemps
64, boulevard Haussmann, 9th – 01 42 82 50 00

THE PERFUMERS WE LOVE:

Maison Francis Kurkdjian
5, rue d'Alger, 1st – 01 42 60 07 07

Greatly inspired by Paris (his micro-shop offers a new look at the rooftops of Paris), Francis Kurkdjian is undoubtedly one of the most gifted fragrance makers of his generation. Of an extreme creativity (scented bubbles, detergents with perfume essences), he offers refined, subtle fragrances for every moment of the day. Pure gems moment of the day. Pure gems in delightful bottles.

Frédéric Malle
21, rue du Mont-Thabor, 1st – 01 42 22 16 89

The Frédéric Malle Edition de Parfum fragrance label features shops, designed by Andrée Putman, offering rare fragrances composed by the world's greatest noses, who are given great creative freedom. The shops are equipped with a "scent column," long Plexiglas tubes you can stand in to breathe in the fragrance emanating all around you.

Serge Lutens
25, rue de Valois, 1st – 01 49 27 09 09

Under the arcades of the Palais-Royal you'll find the shop Serge Lutens, doubtless one of the most beautiful in Paris. Lutens is a versatile, jack-of-all trades talent. His fragrance range is strong, mysterious and captivating. The bottles are beautifully incandescent.

Penhaligon's
209, rue Saint-Honoré, 1st – 01 49 26 91 66

Those who love John Steed and British chic will love this place. Founded in the late 19th century, this august institution that counted the likes of Winston Churchill as a customer offers fragrances and classic, robust, distinguished colognes. A classic barbershop boutique worth seeing in its own right.

L'Artisan Parfumeur
2, rue de l'Amiral-de-Coligny, 1st – 01 44 88 27 50

In 1976 Jean Laporte founded L'Artisan Parfumeur. The idea was to create fragrances to revive the spirit of perfume, honouring natural raw materials (flowers, fruits, spices). These highly original perfumes leave the lion's share of inspiration to their makers, among whom are Jean-Claude Ellena, the "nose" of Hermès. Jean Laporte has since left the hosue to found Maître Parfumeur et Gantier.

ALSO:

Santa Maria Novella (chez Amin Kader)
1, rue de la Paix, 2nd – 01 42 61 33 25

Parfums de Nicolaï
45, rue des Archives, 3rd – 01 48 87 05 19

Lubin
21, rue des Canettes, 6th – 01 43 29 52 42

État Libre d'Orange
69, rue des Archives, 3rd – 01 42 78 30 09

IS PERFUME
ONLY FOR ONE SEX?

Please. If you think fragrances for men exist, you must get that idea out
of your head, once and for all. A fragrance is a fragrance, full stop. You can
douse yourself, like Near Easterners with notes of rose or go out at night
wearing a strange, powdery fragrance that wouldn't have been odd on a
Second Empire tart. Only one thing matters: try the fragrance on your skin,
live with it a little, and above all, wear it proudly. In a word, trust your olfactory
memory and your own tastes.

SHUCKING OYSTERS WITH FRIENDS

"He was a bold man that first eat an oyster."
Jonathan Swift

"*You shouldn't wait too long to shuck oysters. Six dozen is work.***"** That's the signal. You don't need more to call in the army and round up helpers. Then the kitchen will overflow with guys (since Antiquity, shucking oysters has been an affair of men).
Oyster knives of various shapes and colours are passed around. Some are pointed and sleek as Italian daggers; others have wide blades and a handle protected by a swordsman's shield; everyone is equipped, after all these years of spending holidays with friends. Everyone uses a dishrag that will end up wet, dirty and green, and everyone rushes to the sink.

One of your friends always suggests: "How about a little glass of white wine? From his fridge he'll take a Sancerre or a Riesling that has been only half asleep, waiting for the right occasion to present itself. The wine glasses are passed around, everyone takes a sip and gets to work. Each has his own technique, pressing the blade down the middle or through the hinge. The triangular, solid tip of the knife pierces, pivots and with a sharp slice loosens the moorings. The blade scrapes, the shell you throw into the bottom of the sink thumps like a rock. After a few moments, you'd think you were in a factory. It's an ideal assembly line, the kind that doesn't exist, where the work is divided up. Of course, everyone tastes a few oysters, so as to be assured about the quality of the very expensive Utah Beach ones that the Sancerre gives even more of an iodized taste to, relaying their little nutty flavour, like an unexpected gift. Everyone feels good, talks about the coming meal. Everyone is anticipating the dinner, in the atmosphere of a kind of trial-run aperitif with lots of chatter. Then the conversation goes off in various directions, running off freely from glass to glass, oyster shell to oyster shell. Invariably a woman sticks her head into the kitchen. "You all are certainly not getting bored! Everyone looks at one another; she must want a glass of wine. But no. Not right away. A brotherhood has been created at the sink, where the scent of ocean spray and wet towels is heavy. The brotherhood of oyster shuckers.
For men only.

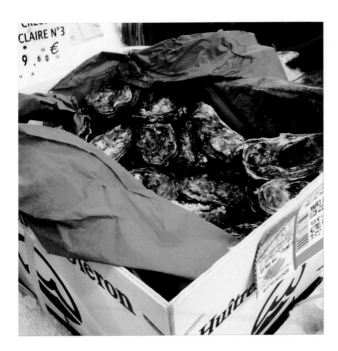

BUY THEM AT:

L'Écume Saint-Honoré
6 rue du Marché Saint-Honoré, 1st
01 42 61 93 87

Jean Quoniam
70 rue Monge, 5th
01 47 07 35 71

Pleine Mer
22 rue de Chabrol, 10th
01 53 34 64 47

Lacroix
44 rue Oberkampf, 11th
01 47 00 93 13

La Dame des huîtres (ATAO)
86 rue Lemercier, 17th
01 46 27 81 12 (tasting possible)

Crusta Poissons
63 rue Duhesme, 18th
01 46 06 78 41

TASTE THEM:

Garnier
111 rue Saint-Lazare, 8th
01 43 87 50 40

L'Écailler du bistrot
22 rue Paul-Bert, 11th
01 43 72 76 77

La Cagouille
10 place Constantin-Brancusi, 14th
01 43 22 09 01

Prunier
16 avenue Victor-Hugo, 16th
01 44 17 35 85 (expensive and beautiful)

L'Huîtrier
16 rue Saussier-Leroy, 17th
01 40 54 83 44

Rech
62 avenue des Ternes, 17th
01 45 72 29 47

Jarrasse
4 avenue de Madrid, Neuilly (92)
01 46 24 07 56

TO GET THE MOST OUT OF THEM

Empty the first bit of water, as it will be reconstituted in the oyster afterwards. Never leave the open shells on a bed of ice, as the cold will neutralize their flavour. It's better to use algae that you've gotten from your oyster shop. For seasoning, never use vinegar, which is too powerful, but only lemon, and sometimes just a touch of ground pepper. Above all, chew!

PATRICK
ROGER

Chocolate Maker, Meilleur Ouvrier de France (France's Best)

LIFE SIZE

In all truth, I like speed. I live at a fast pace, with no time to lose, too much dazzle, too many projects and ideas. Those who know me follow the rhythm and accept the pace that many others find hellish. To get around I use my motorbike. It's quick, obviously. In my chocolate shop, it's the same: if I have an idea, I carry it out, even if I have to spend the night doing it. I instantly want to create what I thought of a moment before.

That doesn't mean I'm unable to spend time enjoying life's small pleasures. It's true that I'm not one to sit around thinking for long; I think fleetingly but intensely. What do I like to do in Paris for fun? Go to the Musée Rodin, and especially the garden. I like to go through it quickly, stop, capture the moment, see what's essential, admire the wonderful life-size exhibitions displayed there. I try to go there regularly, because I really like some of the temporary exhibitions, even if I only stay for a short time. Six minutes are enough. Even there, I have to go quickly! But I must admit that if a soft, fine rain dampens the garden, I'll stroll a few moments longer.

SEE PARIS
AS A PAINTING

The feeling of déjà-vu rises up with the turn of a street, vibrant, unexpected. You stop. The feeling is strong. The walls are tinted with gouache, the skies have the faded look of wash drawings, figures turn to wax. Everything has a smoky pastel look, a look of Impressionist oils on canvas. There is a gleam to the pavement. The geography hovers, becomes flat. It's obvious: Paris is a painting.

Photos: Palais Garnier (Opéra), Notre-Dame, Gare du Nord, Grand Bassin and Jardin des Tuileries, Square du Vert-Galant, the Grands Boulevards and the Boulevard Haussmann.

PLAYING TENNIS OUTDOORS

*"We'll play for fun.
We'll see what happens."*
Kléber Haedens

As soon as the first buds of and warm sunshine of spring come out, you start to feel excited about playing tennis again. In general, you know the French open at Roland-Garros is not far off; you navigate from April and May, when women are again baring their ankles on the street. A little bit of sport wouldn't be bad for your body, still heavy from winter. After all, soon it will have prove itself on the beach. So you take your racket out of its cover, weigh it up, check the tension of the strings with a few strikes against the palm, realign them to form a perfect grid, spin it quickly in your palm to ensure it obeys: you're ready.

A few phone calls later, on a free weekend when you've postponed a lunch, and you head off to the courts. You're all in white – you've set this rule as though loyal to the British spirit of Wimbledon. White, it is true, looks good. You head onto the courts that have been deserted since the first signs of wintry weather. The metal gate clacks shut, metallic, vibrant, attracting the attention of strollers and occupants of the neighbouring court. You warm up, jump a little to awaken your sleeping muscles, choose your side. Mindful of the sunshine (what a soft, sensual feeling to slide your sunglasses into the racket bag), you decide to stay in the shade. The first ball is served.

You'll play like this for a few minutes, but it's not that easy to get your body going again and you feel a bit lost. Your movements are still off the mark. Your breath is short, you don't hurry between exchange to pick up the stray balls. But little by little, it all falls into place and you work up to speed. The euphoria of powerful balls that make a dull characteristic pop when struck takes over and you become taken up in the game. Though the air is still a little chilly, the sunshine beautiful and the breeze gently caressing, you won't forget the double faults, the balls you hit into the net, and the lobs too long to remember, once you're sitting on the bench out of breath, perspiring and thirsty, the feeling of having spent an hour of happiness in your sneakers. That is, tennis shoes.

A FEW NICE COURTS WHERE YOU CAN PLAY IN THE SHADE:

MAIRIE DE PARIS TENNIS COURTS (reservations at **tennis.paris.fr**) :

Fonds des Princes
1, rue du Bois-de-Boulogne, 16th
01 46 51 17 53 (the neighbour of the Roland-Garros stadium)

Tennis du Luxembourg
3, rue Guynemer, 6th
01 43 25 79 18 (Does it still need an introduction? If you're shy, best to forget it.)

Tennis Suzanne Lenglen
2, rue Louis-Armand, 15th
01 44 26 26 50

Tennis La Faluère
113, route de la Pyramide, 12th
01 43 74 40 93 (in the middle of the Bois de Vincennes)

Tennis Aurelle de Paladines
17, boulevard d'Aurelle-de-Paladines, 17th – 01 46 24 27 36

PRIVATE COURTS:

K'fé Court
86, boulevard Flandrin, 16th
01 44 05 11 70

(A restaurant – worth it essentially for its English-style setting – with a huge terrace and adjoining tennis court.)

Tennis Club de Paris
15, avenue Félix-d'Hérelle, 16th
01 46 47 73 90

BARBECUING A RIB ROAST

"Above all my children, do things simply."

Auguste Escoffier

Don't try to find a logical or scientific explanation for this as there is none. Yet every year it's the same thing. With the first buds of spring, the first chirping of birds in the chestnut trees, and the first silk skirts on Rue Montorgueil, your friends in the suburbs ring to make the suggestion. "How about a little barbecue this weekend?" How can you resist? You're looking forward to sniffing the clear, vibrant smell of spring, to tasting cool wine and renewing your acquaintance with life's simple pleasures.

Barbecuing is all of that. Good weather, terraces and gardens, cooking without a kitchen. All you need are the ingredients and the time to cook. Nothing else.

The season is open, and summer will soon be here. This is only the first in a long series of barbecues to come. So you have to be careful; you mustn't screw it up. No question of beef or pork sausage, merguez sausage, or skewers: the dish you're lusting over for this inaugural event, a beautiful rib

roast, never weighs less than 1.5 kilos. Sometimes there are two of them. That's the set menu. You'll also need a dash of oil, a few herbes de Provence, the pepper mill and fleur de sel, nothing more. Barbecued rib roast is not cooking, it's a miracle of nature.

You choose a thick cut of fleshy animal meat that's still a bit bloody in its wax paper. You will cook it on ardent embers for a long time, with patience and desire. You listen to it grill, cook down.

You welcome the aromatic smoke that will give it all its flavour. A huge knife will cut it easily, into thick crackling pieces, turning from brown to red as you reach the middle. The meat eaters in the crowd will give it a hard time, caressing the tempting, opalescent fat with the tip of their forks even as they attack, happily biting into the chewy, char-grilled meat. Till there is none left. There will always be one unscrupulous person to scrape the bone with his Laguiole knife. Me.

BLOODY QUESTIONS
FOR YVES-MARIE LE BOURDONNEC

(Butcher in Asnières)

– What do you ask your butcher when you want a good rib roast?
It's important to know what connection the butcher has with the cattleman, because the quality of the meat depends above all on him. In fact, maturing is one of the essential criteria for it, and how the animal is fed during its lifetime (there should be no fermented fodder and the ration of grain should be balanced). Also, the butcher can let his prime ribs mature a long time, so that the collagen disintegrates and the fat content in the muscle (marbled, veined) is diffused aromatically.

– How do we recognize a quality rib roast?
It must smell like hazelnut, have a texture that holds together (not soft), and the dry fat should be a cream colour (not vacuum packed). It must be able to hold up under the cut with the bone on top without deforming and falling loosely (maturation is optimum). The colour must be dark red. It mustn't drip too much (a little is normal).

– What kind of cattle are best suited to rib roast?
In France, Limousine, Parthenaise or Aubrac, for cows aged 3 to 5 years. More rarely, you can find Normandes or Salers cattle, if they have been raised for meat and not for milking, and even more rarely, the steers aged 3 to 4 years. To illustrate how rare these steers are, you must know that I only find about 10 per year through the grapevine, in Normandy or Poitou. In France, 90% of the red meat we consume is cow.

Avoid the exotic, American Black-Angus that arrives vacuum-packed in 1 °C refrigerated containers (the meat doesn't mature and it's full of water).

– How many grams per person should we ask for?
You have to count 300 to 400 g per person; the bone shouldn't weigh more than 250 g maximum. Ask your butcher to ensure the top part of the rib roast is already removed (it's the long muscle covering the rib roast, often left aside to be sold at the price of the rib.

– What is the ideal thickness?
No thicker than 7 cm for successful cooking.

– How do you cook it in the oven?
Sear it in a skillet with a bit of very hot, neutral oil (grape seed), so that you get a good crust all around it. Sprinkle with salt and pepper. Heat the oven to 220 °C. Leave it in the oven until the roast reaches 50 °C in the middle (check with a thermometer), about 15 to 20 minutes. Take it out of the oven, leave it on a plate and cover it with aluminium foil. Let it sit for 15 minutes.

– How do you barbecue it?
Sear it 1 minute on each side, then 2 minutes on each side, then 4 minutes on each side. Sprinkle it with salt and pepper while it's cooking, and then set it aside covered in aluminium foil for 15 minutes.

TOP QUALITY BUTCHERS:

Boucherie Charcellay
263, rue Saint-Jacques, 5th – 01 43 26 77 23

Boucherie Pascal Duciel
41, avenue de Saxe, 7th – 01 47 34 88 20

Boucheries Nivernaises
99, rue du Faubourg-Saint-Honoré, 8th
01 43 59 11 02

Boucherie Michel
Marché Beauvau
3, place d'Aligre, 12th
01 43 40 62 58

Hugo Desnoyer
45, rue Boulard, 14th – 01 45 40 76 67

Yves-Marie Le Bourdonnec
4, rue Maurice-Bokanowski, Asnières (92)
01 47 93 86 37

MEAT LOVERS' RESTAURANTS:

Robert et Louise
64, rue Vieille-du-Temple, 3rd – 01 42 78 55 89

La Maison de l'Aubrac
37, rue Marbeuf, 8th – 01 43 59 05 14

Unico
15, rue Paul-Bert, 11th – 01 43 67 68 08

Le Severo
16, rue des Plantes, 14th – 01 40 44 73 09

WHERE TO EAT WHAT IN PARIS

Paris in your plate: a little tour of the town in 25 emblematic dishes.

Parmentier of oxtail with truffles
by Guy Martin
at Grand Véfour
17, rue du Beaujolais, 1st
01 42 96 56 27

The pot-au-feu
from La Tour de Montlhéry (Chez Denise)
5, rue des Prouvaires, 1st
01 42 36 21 82

The club sandwich
at L'hôtel Costes
239, rue Saint-Honoré, 1st
01 42 44 50 25

The hake "Colbert"
at La Fontaine Gaillon
1, place Gaillon, 2nd
01 47 42 63 22

The French fries
at Chez Georges
1, rue du Mail, 2nd
01 42 60 07 11

The roast chicken
at L'Ami Louis
32, rue Vertbois, 3rd
01 48 87 77 48

The jarret-marmelade
at La brasserie de l'Île-Saint-Louis
55, quai de Bourbon, 4th
01 43 54 02 59

The duck au sang
at La Tour d'Argent
15, quai de la Tournelle, 5th
01 43 54 23 31

The frogs' legs
at the Moulin à Vent
20, rue des Fossés-Saint-Bernard, 5th
01 43 54 99 37

The salad of pan-sautéed cow's teats
at the Ribouldingue
10, rue Saint-Julien-le-Pauvre, 5th
01 46 33 98 80

The Cesar salad
at the Café de Flore
172, boulevard Saint-Germain, 6th
01 45 48 55 26

The œuf mayonnaise
at the Closerie des Lilas
171, boulevard du Montparnasse, 6th
01 40 51 34 50

The white veal stew
at Aux Charpentiers
10, rue Mabillon, 6th
01 43 26 30 05

The breaded pigs' trotters
at the Comptoir du Relais
9, carrefour de l'Odéon, 6th
01 43 29 12 05

The rice pudding
at L'Ami Jean
27, rue Malar, 7th
01 47 05 86 89

The savoury soufflés
at La Cigale Récamier
4, rue Récamier, 7th
01 45 48 86 58

Hare à la royale
by Éric Fréchon
at Le Bristol's Epicure
restaurant
112, rue du Faubourg-Saint-
Honoré, 8th
01 53 43 43 00

Pigeon 'André Malraux'
at Lasserre
17, avenue Franklin-Roosevelt, 8th
01 43 59 02 13

The calf's head
by Jean-Pierre Vigato
at Apicius
20, rue d'Artois, 8th
01 43 80 19 66

The Paris-Brest dessert
at the Bistrot Paul Bert
18, rue Paul-Bert, 11th
01 43 72 24 01

The pâté en croûte
by Rodolphe Paquin
at Le Repaire de Cartouche
8, boulevard des Filles du Calvaire,
11th
01 47 00 25 86

The sole meunière
at Le Duc
243, boulevard Raspail, 14th
01 43 20 96 30

The whole roasted turbot
at La Grande Cascade
Allée de Longchamp, 16th
01 45 27 33 51

The boneless rib steak with
sauce
at the Relais de Venise
271, boulevard Pereire, 17th
01 45 74 27 97

The roast Camembert
at the Café Burq
6, rue Burq, 18th
01 42 52 81 27

(When you are sure of the right
season – for truffles, game,
scallops, mushrooms – make
sure when you book that the
dish you desire is on the menu.
The dishes suggested are,
unfortunately, subject
to change.)

où manger quoi ?

LE RELAIS DE VENISE

APICIUS

LE BRISTOL

LA GRANDE CASCADE

LASSERRE

L'AMI JEAN

LA CIGA

CAFÉ BURQ

LA FONTAINE GAILLON

HÔTEL COSTES

LE GRAND VEFOUR

LE JEU DU MAIL

CHEZ DENISE

L'AMI LOUIS

LE REPAIRE DE CARTOUCHE

LE CAFÉ DE FLORE

LES CHARPENTIERS

LE RIBOULDINGUE

BRASSERIE DE L'ÎLE ST-LOUIS

LE COMPTOIR DU RELAIS

LA TOUR D'ARGENT

LE BISTROT PAUL-BERT

LE MOULIN A VENT

LA CLOSERIE DES LILAS

LE DUC

PRINTING AND VERGÉ PAPER

"Do you know what it is to write? It's an old, very vague but envious practice, whose meaning lies in the mystery of the heart."
Stéphane Mallarmé

Sometimes you like to slip quietly into an anachronism. To walk to work, listen to an Offenbach operetta by the light of an upright piano, put on a red silk sweater, throw a punch at someone over a question of honour. Or even, write a letter.

What wonderful delights the written word can offer. There is one custom you'd like to keep up, to keep from going down the drain along with so much else: the thank you note. You come back from a weekend, an evening, even a lunch, and full of the moment, at the peak of emotion, you write your thanks in the form of a small note. Not a text message (though it is a lesser evil), but a real note with letters formed with the ink of a fountain pen, either in black or the blue of the South seas, or violet. You enjoy getting the ink to glide over the vergé paper of a beautiful card, in the re-found, old-fashioned joy of a formal note of thanks.

You've waited for your wide-margined cards for a long time. On them is a name and address, like a storefront, printed in English letters. You've chosen the thickness, colour (why not mouse grey paper?), layout and fonts. All that's left is to approve the engraved plate, then plunge back into the fury of modern life, waiting patiently. You cool your heals, pretending not to think about it any longer. Finally one day, the boxes are there before you.

You untie the coloured ribbon with the printer's name on it, take off the cover and slide the tissue back to uncover the first card.

You pick it up, and your urge to slide your thumb over the printed name at the top and feel the relief is stronger than anything. Now, you just have to find the right pen.

Everything else is just literature.

EMMANUEL
RUBIN

Journalist,
Editor-in-Chief, L'Optimum

LE TRAIN BLEU

It appears that to love, you have to know how to leave. As though from afar, you indulge in the feeling of absence, regrets and fantasies. Yet as is often the case for men, I have no talent for separations. With Paris, it's worse. I feel like dropping it but am never brave enough to abandon it. Consequently, I hide behind the invisible sheet of a double life, with hardly more courage than to choose the randomness of a train station, because a station makes you feel like leaving and coming back, so they say. Gare de Lyon is even better. With complete impunity, it offers a staircase totally suited to any good adulterer. At the top of the stairs, beneath a neon sign that surely witnessed a few good slaps in the face, behind heavy curtains now bored from having been pulled so many times, is the restaurant Le Train Bleu. Monumental. Historical. The dining room is as big as the platform area. The banquettes are laid out like Pullman cars. On the walls and ceiling are Pompier style paintings that become excessively pyromaniac in stoking the allegorical fires of travelling. In the back, the Tunisien and the Algérien dining rooms still seem to await the lot of legionnaires. And at every table, stories are told and memories shared of Colette and Jean Gabin, but there is no one to tell you where Maréchal Pétain usually dined. Table 92 is my favorite. When Luc Besson filmed his *Nikita*, this is where Anne Parillaud came. You have the feeling you're dining on her lap. At Le Train Bleu, even the toilets are part of the game. "You can piss there while watching the trains pull out," said Salvador Dalí, whom we know also had a thing for train stations. Obviously the food, an expression of laborious comfort, contents itself with being the third wheel. As though it always knew you didn't come here for it. Le Train Bleu is my railway bordello. I deceive Paris right inside Paris, in dreams of departure and in eyes of the passersby. I am cowardly, but faithful.

HEAD IN THE CLOUDS

"Clouds are wonderful nurses."
Christian Bobin

Since the present sometimes weighs on us, and the law of gravity seems universal and makes heavy trucks of our bodies, you have to know how to look up. Leave the realm of immediacy and take a bit of distance. Become absorbed in the moment, watching the clouds race by.

Most of the time, we don't give much thought to clouds. They hang out in groups and make their way to the horizon, breaking up around the towers of Notre-Dame cathedral, stretching their white scarves over the Seine. It's no use for them to break speed records or to pile up into enormous balloon shapes, since no one is paying attention. Tired of so much indifference, suddenly here they are. They swell up, steel grey, and toss out their lightning. It could really rain! They are threatening. Finally the masses realize they exist. Which is sad, because what the masses ignore or neglect, is that Paris is the city of light. There are always improbable, incredibly beautiful, breathtakingly violent skies here. Filled with light.

So yes, you have to raise your eyes. You have to like clouds. Like their vaporous, Chantilly cream shapes. Let the pearl grey melt into the virginal whiteness, onto a sky-blue background. Live with your head in a Constable painting.

WHERE TO LOOK UP

Clouds are a matter of nature. So to see them we'll choose parks and flowery spots, gardens where seated on your bench, you'll have the uncontrollable reflex to put your head back and look up. They are also a question of seasons. Changing skies, sudden showers and clouds bursting into storm. Spring and autumn reign supreme over the uniformly white summer sky or the boring smoky grey sky of winter.

To find them, you have to go where the city is flat, where the views crash against the horizon. For me nothing is better than the moving sky over the Place de la Concorde, sliding toward the Tuileries. But sometimes all you need is a little glimpse. Even a narrow street where the hard blue sky creates a cover with the sudden trace of a passing cloud.

What's important is to hold your head up. To forget nothing of the sky's immensity. Like a permanent reminder of beauty.

WATER IN MY WHISKY

"I knew a Polish woman who drank a little for breakfast. You have to admit: it's really a drink for men."

Michel Audiard *(Les Tontons Flingueurs)*

We're never wary enough of discussions that drag on and on. They take you to distant destinations and, often, to unexpected ones. We've deserted the dining room table, where the cake leftovers display their nightly boredom among the rumpled napkins. No one wants to separate; you just want to find a more comfortable position, stretch your legs and continue the conversation. So you slide the little iPod button to the quietest tracks, then you open the bar. It's time for strong liquor and the herb tea mug.

These old whiskies. You cuddle them; they show their mettle only after midnight. They have exotic names (Laphroaig, Balvenie, Talisker) from the upper latitudes, labels like invitation cards, and at the bottom, eau-de-vie that dances in the golden reflections. You pour just a touch into each glass (in a cognac glass, which is how I like to drink it) and you already feel the aromas of the moors and heaths, smell the gray smoke rising to the nostrils. You stir the liquid a little and other fragrances appear. You add a drop of mineral water to increase the aromas tenfold, then, you finally risk it, taking small sips.

The first invades your mouth like a charge from the Scots Guards. The aromas spread through it, and with the powerful, peat-like taste, all of Scotland disembarks: wet boots, stone walls, valleys and lakes, old towers covered in vegetation, the iodine of the islands, the grouse hunt. You no longer speak.

You are elsewhere, all together, carried off far from here.

It's silly. You haven't got your umbrellas.

THE BEST PLACES FOR SINGLE MALTS:

La Maison du Whisky
20, rue d'Anjou, 8th – 01 42 65 03 16

Caves Augé
116, boulevard Haussmann, 8th – 01 45 22 16 97

Caves de Courcelles
206 bis, rue de Courcelles, 17th – 01 47 64 97 79

JUST A SIP, PLEASE.

Balvenie
Aged 12 years. Distilled in 100+ year-old stills, and aged in round, mild sherry barrels.

Lagavulin
Aged 16 years. Think peat, magnificent with a Havana.

Springbank
Aged 15 years. From one of the last family distilleries; powerful and highly aromatic.

Talisker
Aged 10 years. The only whisky from the Isle of Skye, with marine notes marked by the iodine of sea spray.

THE BRA STRAP AT LUNCH

"Violent love can only subsist with a vast, ardent imagination."
Stendhal

I absolutely have to think of something else. Quickly. I'm making an immense effort not to let anything show, but it feels that every movement I make and every look I take betray me. Yet everything started out fine; the lunch was to be totally carefree, professional but not overly so, a first meeting just to meet the person for possible future business reasons. She had delicately placed herself opposite me, across the table. She was a young woman of no particular charm, with big eyes ringed in black eyeliner, the nose a bit heavy, and an air of someone straight out of an operetta, her smile fixed and too easy. Her skirt was thrown over long brownish boots, her top a little knit sweater decently low-cut, without being provocative, yet well revealing the shoulders to highlight a rather small bust. The season's new entries had ended in a swirl of mutual presentations, and shortened and embellished resumes many times presented. The business lunch routine. There was nothing personal about it. It was all about experience, jobs, a position.

The moustachioed waiter – wonderful English butler-style whiskers – had left the main course on the table. I was quietly dissecting the cod; she was working away at her fillet of veal with her Laguiole knife. It was the world in reverse, as it happens in Paris. It was while she was going into

detail about her biggest clients that suddenly, it appeared! There, just at her collarbone, at the edge of her too-pale shoulder: her bra strap. An unlikely, unexpected ribbon. Lace caressing her skin, in view of all.

So now I'm off – so easily – because of this little bit of light-blue fabric. It's impossible for me to take my eyes off it. Whatever I do, they can't stop being subjected to the absurd attraction of this incongruous presence. I hardly listen to her. Confused, I give my opinion at moments and let her tell me all about her files. My concentration frays, as fast as I empty my glass of Pouilly. The emotion that makes my head spin is delightful, because unexpected. My eyes linger, pass from a bit of innocently provocative fabric to her long hair caressing her neck. And the entire lunch goes off on a tangent. It's just a detail, of course, but the kind of detail that turns the tide, or the tablecloth, with a violent surge of intense pleasure. I swallow a mouthful of lukewarm fish; she suddenly appears desirable to me. A woman. A body. I look at her hands, her fine wrists, and inexorably along her bare arms toward the shoulder and the origin of my distress. I feel a little ridiculous, and yet . . .

HAVING A SUIT MADE

"You say fashion? I must warn you right away about it.
Launch it if you can, but never follow it. You must not be in style.
The real Parisian is the one who is behind the fashions
by about 15 years – or ahead of it by 15 days."
Sacha Guitry

You can try to think it is of no significance. That you don't care at all. That other things are important, and not things like appearances. Of course. But because you do have to wear clothes, why not do it with style? Philippe Noiret understood this well, remarking mischievously that "life being short" it was better "to travel in first class." And thus, with class. Because to display your personality and taste through a suit is a kind of freedom, of independence. Choosing beauty and elegance is the ultimate politeness.

Armed with this bit of philosophy about fashion and suits, you enter the shop of the person you've chosen to become "your" tailor. The choice is difficult, and you want it to be objective but in the end, it comes down to a smile, a friendly remark, a skill you judge with a wet fingertip and mainly from the look of the suits hanging there, awaiting the visit of the future owners. You are now one of them, trotting back for the first try, sucking in your abdomen a bit, and your eyes on the lookout. What will this suit be like, whose navy blue fabric you've chosen from a sample hardly any bigger than a Moleskin notebook and whose shape you've defined in purely arbitrary fashion? Two buttons, straight collar, ticket pocket, red lining.

They bring it out to you; you try it on, come back to the mirror. Here it is, this one-of-a-kind suit, an outfit that is your reflection, a state of mind, a calling card. There's a surprise as soon as you have the jacket on: it is so well fitted that you don't feel it. Nothing weighs on your shoulders, nothing pulls at your muscles. This suit is a dream, an illusion of wool. The fabric has the softness of one of Salome's veils; it falls perfectly, without the least crease. You open the jacket, have the scarlet lining flamed, count the inside pockets, note with delight the little slit, a hiding place you alone are aware of. The secret pleasure of made-to-measure suits.

They say the devil is in the details. Often happiness is, too.

OFF-THE-RACK? SEMI-FINISHED? MADE-TO-MEASURE? BESPOKE?

It's difficult to untangle the threads of these terms, which are recognized more or less, since tailors themselves have a worrying tendency to blur the lines, creating a bit of confusion as to the differences between them. So what do you do the first time you head off into the pell-mell of pins and measuring tape?

Let's keep things simple. We'll only distinguish between bespoke (the true bespoke, nec plus ultra of elegance, at extremely high prices) and semi-finished (the most common suit, called through wrong usage of language "made-to-measure"), the other differences coming from the quality of materials and the tailoring. So bespoke consists in hand-making a one-of-a-kind pattern, specifically adapted to your morphology, thus distinguished from the semi-finished suit, where (and this is a lot already) alterations only, to an existing pattern, are made based on your measurements.

Let's explain the steps that should lead you one day to the Most Holy Place.

You'll become initiated into the world of tailored suits with a semi-finished suit, called "off-the-rack." Here a standard pattern will be altered to your measurements, with a limited choice of "options" (number of pockets, type of collar, buttons, lining) and using fabrics from low- to the midrange. The quality of the finished product and the finishing details will largely depend on the know-how of the maker and obviously, on the price. Generally the measurements taken in this type of store are done by a sales clerk who is hardly ever a tailor. So in choosing your shop in this category, you really have to be extremely vigilant. Count on spending between €300 and €700 to have a suit made.

Now having sensed the pleasure of getting your suit fitted, you'll probably want to move even farther ahead with your requirements. You'll logically turn to hand-tailored semi-finished (or made-to-measure suits). Again, an existing pattern will be adapted but the choice of patterns, higher quality fabrics and possible finishing details (often done by hand) will be larger. Here a real tailor will look after your needs, and he will increase the measuring points and the observations based on experience, about your needs. Count between €700 €2,000 for a suit.

Finally, if your tastes and needs require it, you can also go to see a bespoke tailor, where by definition anything is possible. However this will cost you at least €3,000 (ouch).

Obviously, the differences between them are not as waterproof as a Barbour jacket, and some tailors offer made-to-measure and bespoke suits to their customers.

YOU'LL FIND A GOOD FIT WITH THESE TAILORS

**OFF-THE-RACK
SEMI-FINISHED:**

Samson
16, boulevard Raspail, 7th
01 45 48 80 65

Gambler (Didier Azoulay)
4, rue de l'Arcade, 8th
01 42 65 41 49

Handson
14, rue Chauveau-Lagarde, 8th
01 42 68 01 28

Wicket
61, boulevard Malesherbes, 8th
01 42 94 19 78

Smuggler
11, avenue Mozart, 16th
01 45 24 65 58

Torcello
134, rue Cardinet, 17th
01 43 80 35 36

**HAND-TAILORED
SEMI-FINISHED,
OR MADE-TO-MEASURE:**

Michael Ohnona
1, rue de Marivaux, 2nd
Pas de téléphone

David Diagne
58, rue des Mathurins, 8th
01 44 56 97 88

Kees Van Beers
44, rue Laffitte, 9th
01 44 63 02 15

Julien Scavini
06 14 90 17 45 (by appointment)

Antoine Jaeger
06 59 97 86 60 (by appointment)

BESPOKE:

Marc Di Fiore
29, rue de Tournon, 6th
01 43 54 67 95

Arnys
14, rue de Sèvres, 7th
01 45 48 76 99

Pape
4, avenue Rapp, 7th
01 47 53 04 05

Cifonelli
33, rue Marbeuf, 8th
01 43 59 39 13

Camps de Lucas
11, place de la Madeleine, 8th
01 42 65 42 15

Djay
9, rue du Chevalier-de-Saint-
Georges, 8th – 01 45 61 99 02

COOKING
SUNDAY LUNCH

"Cooking presupposes the cook will have a light head, a generous spirit and a big heart."
Paul Gauguin

On Sunday morning you always get off to a late start, but it doesn't matter. Time passes more slowly then, which is doubtless why you choose lazy music: Chet Baker and the alley-cat squawk of his trumpet. You woke up a little later than usual; the children are still in their pyjamas in the living room. In the fridge and on the kitchen table are the things you've bought at the market: seasonal vegetables from the market gardener you like from the Perche region, asparagus from Sologne, two big line-caught sea bass, fresh from the coast of Normandy, that the fish merchant charges the price of gold for. It's not that important after all. It's not Sunday every day. And today, as is custom, Dad is the one in the kitchen.

So there you are bent over the counter, Chet Baker softly murmuring his "time after time," the ingredients like a still life. The first thing you enjoy is taking inventory. Everything is there at hand, the food, spices and utensils. You won't do anything too complicated. You're not there to wow your friends one evening but make your family happy by cooking for them, with no fancy tricks. The seasons dictate the musts: simmering dishes in winter, such as pot-au-feu, beef-bourguignon or white veal stew, grilled meats or fish in summer, roast chicken, tomato and mozzarella salad, small red mullets. Sometimes, in spite of all, you're in a hurry. So you season some pasta with a bit of this and that (asparagus tips, peas, artichokes) and happiness slips into your plate in less than 10 minutes.

Today there is a maritime feel to things, so you'll roast these fish, lightly placed on a bed of crunchy vegetables, soaking up vapours of lemon. One of your children often comes in because he wants to see, learn, help. The Sunday kitchen is the school of taste. What you like in this room in the back, a refuge of wood, ceramic and lacquer, is the feeling of escape, where your thoughts dissolve into gestures as you busy yourself with concocting a good little meal. No more worries, no more obligations, nothing but the present, the aromas and savours, the tender, colourful life of a Sunday recipe. Time slows down, filled with smells and memories, the taste of your grandparents' generous cuisine, so nourishing in affection. It's a comfy, ancestral thing you can't explain.

So you take your time. Does it matter if you don't sit down at the table until 1:30? You'll go out for a walk later, cut the naptime for the little ones, choose a film at teatime and then let the late afternoon finish up with a book or board game. The evening will come, and along with it, the week ahead, trying to stick its nose in already. Time continues on its way, hurrying you into the night.

True. Tomorrow is already Monday.

QUICK, GOOD AND EASY SUNDAY RECIPES

For a winter Sunday:
MY WHITE VEAL STEW

Buy some sauté of veal and store it at room temperature. Slice two carrots into rounds, and mince a large handful of mushrooms. In an iron pot, sauté an onion and two cloves of garlic cut into big pieces in a pat of butter and some olive oil, until the onion becomes translucent. Put the veal into the pot and stir it until all the pieces are whitened, but not browned. Add a crumbled up half-cube of chicken broth. Add pepper and sprinkle with a bit of cumin. Cover with a mix of two-thirds white wine, one-third water. Add carrots and mushrooms. Put the lid back on the pot and cook on medium to low fire, for about an hour or an hour and a half, stirring regularly. Once the meat is cooked and tender, thicken the sauce. To do so, dissolve a tablespoon of cornflour in a bowl containing a bit of cold water. Add a ladle of hot broth from the pot into the bowl, mix then pour it all into the pot. Mix everything with the meat, adding two tablespoons of fresh cream. Continue cooking for five more minutes, to let the sauce take on the right consistence (if necessary, repeat the corn flour step). Serve directly from the pot with an accompaniment of rice or pasta that soaks up the sauce, like pipe rigate or rigatoni.

Ingredients
Good quality sauté of veal, two carrots, a handful of mushrooms, an onion, two cloves of garlic, whole cumin seeds, a bottle of white wine, a half-cube of chicken broth, cornflour, fresh cream, pepper, butter, olive oil.

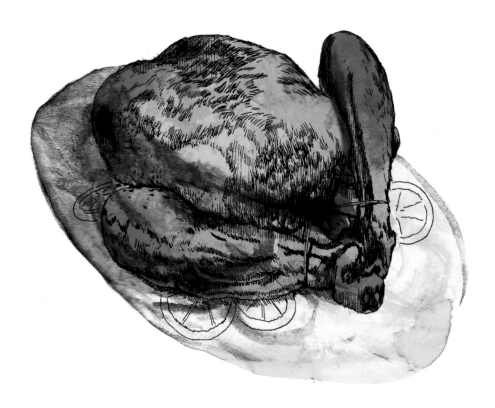

For a summer Sunday:
CHICKEN WITH LEMON AND CORIANDER

Choose a big free-range chicken, leave it out at room temperature. Heat the oven to 180 °C. Cut a lemon into four pieces. Garnish the inside of the chicken with two of the pieces then add a few slices of ginger and a bouquet of fresh coriander. Set aside a few branches of coriander. Pour two glasses of white wine into an oven pan, with an onion cut into big pieces, and two garlic cloves cut into tiny pieces. Place the chicken on the pan. Squeeze the juice from the last lemon pieces all over it. Slash the flanks of the drumsticks with a knife. Put a few pats of butter on the thighs and breasts. Sprinkle with salt and paper. Place in the oven and let it cook for a good 2 hours at 180°C (the secret to keeping the meat tender is cooking it for a long time at a low temperature), basting regularly. Serve with a dash of cut coriander leaves.

Ingredients
A farm-range chicken, two organic lemons, one bunch of coriander, one small stick of ginger, two cloves of garlic, one onion, two glasses of white wine, salt, pepper, butter.

CHARLES
DANTZIG
Writer, Editor

WHAT I ENJOY DOING IN PARIS

If you're in the Jardin des Tuileries in fine weather and you see a pair of long legs sticking out from a low chair and resting on the edge of one of the big ornamental ponds, and a book or newspaper hiding a face, there's a strong chance it will be me. I also like the little basin at the Palais-Royal, but the temptations there distract me. A bookstore. A few clothing stores. The memory of writers who lived in the place or set their novels there, and whose ranks I've just joined by setting several scenes of my last book at the nearby Le Nemours café. As I'm distracted, I make appointments there. "What about meeting at the Palais-Royal?" The big pond at the Tuileries is for abstract thoughts and solitude. I sit with my back to the Rue de Rivoli. The pond is big with its thin foutain, the wide sky of Paris, no monuments, or practically none, in sight, and hardly anything but the little boats of the children to distract me a moment by making me think of paintings from 1880. Apart from them, there are no images. Reading and myself, without myself. Ah, it is evening, is it not? How I'd have liked daylight savings time, when the sun, going down . . .

GIVING JEWELLERY TO A PRETTY WOMAN

"With every movement you heard silver clinking at her wrists. "
Serge Gainsbourg

Giving jewellery to a pretty woman is a pleasure you look forward to. You imagine her surprise, her smile, the emotion, her fingers pulling at the ribbon of the little dark box that you've slid towards her, nonchalantly, at the restaurant. You think of how her face will brighten, how she'll try it on right away. Then the sweet kiss, in thanks.

So here you are, walking through the aisles of a department store, going from one display case to another. You follow the lustre of gold or silver, leaving behind the costume jewellery style of plastic, the original look of crystal. You turn up your nose at the grandiloquent, disdain the flashy. Will it be a necklace? A choker? A light chain like a ribbon around her neck, for the graceful base of her slender nape and a little jewel sliding into her cleavage. Or a long necklace? With spheres, beads, cubes, or a long thread of silver sliding down the shoulders to the tummy in several successive rings, like a slightly crazy touch from the 1920s.

A ring? Rare, precious stones? A solitaire? Though it's not quite "the" big moment. A bracelet? Yes, a bracelet. You never think of it. Decorating her wrists, embellishing them with vibrant, noisy touches. So you think of the fine chains that are such feminine signs of distinction and elegance. Here is one, a large polished silver one that will give her the look of a Greek goddess in the sunshine. It has a bit of nacre, and mat reflections. It's a seasonal bracelet that

THE OUT-OF-THE-ORDINARY
JEWELS WOMEN ADORE:

Aurélie Bidermann
At Colette – 213, rue Saint-Honoré, 1st
01 55 35 33 90

Philippe Tournaire
7, place Vendôme, Cour Vendôme, 1st
01 40 20 00 19

Delfina Delettrez
At Podium – 334, rue Saint-Honoré, 1st
09 64 07 46 57

Lorenz Bäumer
4, place Vendôme, 1st
01 42 86 99 33

Dinh Van
16, rue de la Paix, 2nd
01 42 61 74 49

Anne Defromont
6, passage du Grand-Cerf, 2nd
01 40 26 70 92

Ela Stone
79, rue des Saints-Pères, 6th
01 45 48 02 54

Ginette NY
At Le Bon Marché – 24, rue de Sèvres, 7th
01 44 39 80 00

Pomellato
66, rue du Faubourg Saint-Honoré, 8th
01 42 65 62 07

will be resplendent on suntanned skin.
The pleasure lies in imagining her the
way we dream of her.

You could also choose a jeweller
on the Place Vendome, a place
fragrant with cut flowers, where the
conversations are low-voiced and the
carpet silky. There the pieces can be
brought out to you on a tray. Take delight
in the fine, white-gloved hand of the
person showing you the items. Ask her
to try the jewellery for you. It looks good
on her, on her coppery arms, so you
think it will look good on the other her.
You look at the price one last time
and tell yourself it's of no importance.
You always end up spending more than
reason allows, it's just how it is. But
then, who's talking about reason?

WALKING IN PARIS

"Getting lost . . . It's what children, lovers and mystics dream about, a dream inaccessible to people travelling with railroad tickets and bank notes. "
Paul Morand

Paris is the city of voluntary disappearances: getting lost there is a vocation. It's a never-ending experience of sheer delight; a privilege that hasn't been abolished, that's reserved for people who know how to go about it. And it's not that difficult. Every season, every hour of the day and night and every mood offers its narrow streets, forgotten nooks and crannies, its avenues as wide as cemeteries. A city of pedestrians, Paris is a series of villages, a tangle of landscapes and layers of centuries. Strolling through it is a journey in itself, and its only cost is the time you put into it.

There is something for every mood, whether you're feeling nostalgic, adventurous, modernist, botanical or industrial. From the memorable façades of the Ile Saint-Louis to the Pont de l'Europe overlooking the misty railway tracks of the Gare Saint-Lazare, from the horsemen's alleys of the Parc de Bagatelle to the Bollywood experience of the Rue du Faubourg-Saint-Denis, it's easy to find the mirror of your soul here.

A city only really gives itself to passersby, to pedestrians who'll take the time to seek it out. On its riverbanks, in its gardens and parks, in the shadow of its cut-stone buildings, the tumult of its markets, the quiet of its cemeteries, the edges of its railways and the slopes of its hills, it reveals itself to the person whose foot falls to the beat of its heart. To the patient person who's curious to see it.

You can walk through it alone or with another person, but rarely more.

Perhaps with a few foreigners or good-natured visitors. Then the city unfolds as we walk, rolling out its dark tapestry and pale façades all sliding past along the river as thick as a country soup.

You must be careful to choose your departure point (the destination is one you will discover as you go, it will be an adventure), and in your pockets you'll take a creased old map, or a Smartphone and its maps, but you'll sacrifice nothing to hikers (no walking shoes, please) and you'll travel light: no backpack, just a bit of change in your pockets to buy a drink, an umbrella in uncertain weather, and a camera for real enthusiasts. Head off aimlessly and without a deadline. Leave for one hour and come back in the very early morning, letting the city take you into its quarters, and showing no resistance. Take your time.

Strolling is an art. It can't be said enough. It's beginning to be a lost art and it's a shame. Some of us are keeping up the fight. I am one of them.

STROLLS THROUGH PARIS

"In Paris, you can lose track of time in the most delightful ways; but you can never lose your way."
Oscar Wilde

HAVING LUNCH ALONE

"Happiness is a solitary exercise."
Jean Anouilh

In summer of course you'll choose a shady corner in the open air, away from the noise of forks. In autumn you'll invariably go back inside one of these bistros, whose clientele is unchanging and where you can so easily make yourself at home. However make no mistake. You cannot improvise when you have lunch alone. The exercise requires a bit of preparation and just as much application. You can't just jump onto the first bit of fast food that comes along, or run to the corner bar/tobacconist (though you might) or the trendiest new organic restaurant that's a big hit in women's magazines. You need warm weather, life around but life at a slow pace, measured and discreet. You need the vague activity going on in the background, which only makes its way to you through the smile of the waitress who's come to take your order.

Today you are lunching alone. It's not a punishment; on the contrary, it's an egotistical pleasure. You're finally enjoying being alone, far from the world, with no need for conversation, and a good book to read. So into your jacket pocket when you set out, you'll have been careful to place a novel, of the right size, or a book of poetry, for days made for languishing. No newspaper, because you want to live the trepidations of the real world behind for a moment. After that, anything is good: a detective novel, a major classic, an adventure story or a sentimental one. But there's just one thing: no book with fragile bindings, because you know that such books will be put to task. You'll hold it in one day, your thumb firmly pressing it down the middle to keep it wide open, which is fatal for beautiful books.

You'll choose the dish that best accompanies your reading. No salads that will toss things indiscreetly out at you; no steak you'll have to cut, since you'd have to put your book down too much; nothing you have to eat with your fingers. So you'll play with the idea of matching meals to books: Simenon goes well with *blanquette de veau*, Maupassant takes you straight to fish, San Antonio calls for beef stew with carrots, and for Verlaine's poetry, only a delicate meal will do. I have this nostalgia for having reading Colette (*Chéri*, I think), practically beneath her windows, on the terrace of the Restaurant du Palais-Royal, the smell of risotto with asparagus all around me. A sweet moment, as though the entire Belle Époque was looking over my shoulder.

SEASONAL SOLITUDE

SPRING

Jaja
3, rue Sainte-Croix-de-la-
Bretonnerie, 4th
01 42 74 71 52

Café Louis Philippe
66, quai de l'Hôtel-de-
Ville, 4th
01 42 72 29 42

Café Guitry
10, place Édouard-VII, 9th
01 40 07 00 77

SUMMER

**Café
du musée Rodin**
77, rue de Varenne, 7th
01 44 18 61 10

Bagatelle
Route de Sèvres à Neuilly,
16th – 01 40 67 98 29

Bal Café
6, impasse de la Défense,
18th – 01 44 70 75 51

AUTUMN

L'Épi d'Or
25, rue Jean-Jacques-
Rousseau, 1st
01 42 36 38 12

Le Timbre
3, rue Sainte-Beuve, 6th
01 45 49 10 40

L'Assiette
181, rue du Château, 14th
01 43 22 64 86

WINTER

Le Chenin
33, rue Le Peletier, 9th
01 47 70 12 01

Chaumette
7, rue Gros, 16th
01 79 97 32 66

Le Petit Salé
99, avenue des Ternes,
17th – 01 40 68 95 09

WINDING YOUR WATCH

*"The time of mankind
is eternity skewed."*
Jean Cocteau

You wind your watch without thinking; it's a habit of yours, once you are all cleaned up, wandering about in your shirtsleeves in the bedroom, and Paris is still but a rumour outside. You awaken the hands of the watch as though they're on a revolving door racing speedily towards the hour of the day, whether exact or approximate. Then there is the meticulous movement of your thumb and index finger on the winder; it takes at least 50 turns to start the day.

You wind it in the evening also, when you step out with your old Swiss ticker, a toggle watch with a number etched on the back, which you've taken out of its mahogany box. It has certainly experienced many a special evening – restaurants, conversations, never-ending adventures. Its fine hands have travelled to faraway lands, seen strange skies.

You awaken it from sleep and bring it to life in a few moments. And everything can start again.

How do you derive satisfaction from such anonymous objects? They're constantly moving, always on time, and never tired. You slip them onto your wrist robotically every morning, without thinking about it. No, what you like are watches of character, which require your attention and know how to get it: the watch face that attracts the eye. They are so dependent. Economical. They sleep as soon as you separate yourself from them. They wake up for just the amount of time you need: a day, an evening, a trip; they don't go to waste. With your eyes on them, as you wind them, you can't not notice how beautiful they are. It's part of their coquetry.

Yet, they don't require much. A bit of attention, a mechanical gesture, almost a caress. And there they are, awake, fragile companions of passing time. They seem to whisper: "Don't forget me." How could we?

THE HAIRSTYLIST'S HANDS

"It's also like those singular caresses that invented a more intense pleasure inside of pleasure itself."
Paul-Jean Toulet

The enamel of the sink is cold and biting against my neck. It's like gunfire, three shots and the curtain rises. Then I feel her hand on my forehead, the clear sound of warm water falling and waves tumbling down my hair. Like a first experience of torpor that relaxes the body and leads to abandon.

One hand under the head. Then the fragrance of shampoo like a balm, its coolness as opposed to the warmth of the water. Her long, fine fingers can begin their dance. The foam rustles a little, like crepe paper you crumple lightly with firm fingers. Speaking of which, fingers are now making a series of precise, enveloping movements in a well-defined path along the top of your head, neck and temples, applying pressure and making circular movements, ten fingers coordinated in a synchronized water ballet.

They're all I feel. The noises of the salon have become distant, I no longer hear a thing. I am here only to follow the trace of these hands that seem to so well know the licentious secrets of my wet head.

I don't ever want this to end. I want to fall asleep softly under the influence of these caresses. I promise, I will never again say a bad word about shampooers, they caress your soul candidly, light the silent fires of Bengal along your spine, and take you elsewhere, a bit of soap and water your only luggage.

It's the little miracle they perform daily.

HAIRSTYLISTS YOU CAN TRUST WITH YOUR . . . HEAD:

David Mallett
14 rue Notre-Dame-des-Victoires, 2nd
01 40 20 00 23

Desfossé
19 avenue Matignon, 8th – 01 43 59 95 13

Jean-Michel Faretra
21 avenue George V, 8th – 01 47 23 01 16

Les Chevelus
44 rue des Martyrs, 9th – 01 48 74 15 45

Meloz Coiffeurs (Philippe Carlier)
11 rue Fontaine, 9th – 01 40 82 99 71

Monsieur
47 rue de la Tour d'Auvergne, 9th
01 45 26 78 25

Ultra
3 rue Saint-Sabin, 11th – 01 43 57 42 67

Mario Lopes
88bis avenue Mozart, 16th – 01 45 27 37 30

Angel
76 rue Pierre Demours, 17th – 01 42 27 60 60

FRANCK
BARANGER

Chef, Head of the restaurant Le Pantruche

SUNDAY MARTYR

I like Paris and its neighbourhoods and the habits you pick up there, the feeling of belonging to a sort of tribe. Mine is "So Pi." It's what I enjoy on Sunday morning, and it's become a ritual. I go up the Rue des Martyrs. And in espadrilles, no less!

It always starts the same way: on the corner of Rue des Martyrs and Rue Choron, I have the first espresso of the morning. It's a way of getting prepared. It's afterwards that the serious part starts. The first stop on the walk is the newsstand. I skim through every magazine that attracts my attention, then I hesitate, I compare them, and I always leave with the same newspaper for myself and women's magazines for her (I thumb through it then always close it with a sigh, not at all understanding the enthusiasm).

Then I head to the fish shop or the butcher, depending on my mood and what's on display. I take turns at each place, getting inspiration for easy recipes that will be a feast for my friends. Then cheese of course. I always buy too much. And if you say cheese, you have to get bread... And for that I go to Landemaine, asking for *"deux baguettes tradition pas trop cuites"* and a delicious *pain au chocolat*. And finally, almost at the top of the street, is the wine store on the Rue des Martyrs. They always give great advice and they are really nice.

And because it's Sunday, and it's always a pleasure, I get up the courage and valiantly go to the end of the Avenue Trudaine, to my friend Bruno's flower shop. He makes bouquets for restaurants, and his good ideas always make my return home a cause for applause. So when I finish up my walk where I began it, with an espresso, croissant, and toasted baguette, and my "voici" and their "voici," it's almost as a hero, worthy of a man of Pantruche. Happiness. In top form once again, I go home, arms loaded down, satisfied and filled with the wonderful feeling of having done my errands. And done them well.

TO MARKET, WITH YOUR LITTLE KIDS

"There was fish, there was butter, there was fowl, there was meat. A volley of bells rang out, creating a stir in the just-opening markets."
Émile Zola

Paris is a village. Or rather, several. From Batignolles to Ménilmontant, the Butte-aux-Cailles to the Eglise d'Auteuil and winding gently over the little mount of Montmartre, Paris has something rustic about it that folds out from Palais-Royal. The people who live in these areas, the provincial people of Paris, have their little habits: references they forged long before, that they stick to fiercely. Take the markets, for example. The market is the ever-ticking heart of a neighbourhood, where locals recognize each other from the size of their shopping bags, their haircut or the jacket they're wearing. You'll find bourgeois/media peeps along the Avenue de Saxe, organic-loving bobos at the Marché des Enfants-Rouges, and sharp, talkative types in the shadow of Métro Barbès.

A Parisian loves his market like he loves his public park: with the sedentary fidelity usually reserved for weekends. He likes the crowd, the buzzing beehive. A market is lively: you run into people you know, you hurry, haggle, fraternize in the queue while awaiting your turn to order aubergine and courgettes, Sainte Maure-de-Touraine and Saint-Nectaire cheese. On rainy days you buy a handful of mushrooms and wild game hanging

MY PREFERRED MARKETS:

3rd: Marché des Enfants-Rouges
(every day, except Monday)
Along the Rue de Bretagne, it's a small, beautiful spot (the oldest market in Paris), but a tad expensive. An ideal place to let the morning slip by, because you can find rather nice little places to eat there.

6th: Marché Raspail
(Tuesday, Friday and Sunday)
This was the precursor to Paris's organic markets. It's loaded with customers, not cheap, and is a gathering of very fine artisans (cheese makers, fruit and market gardeners).

7th: Marché Saxe-Breteuil
(Thursday and Saturday)
Chic but inexpensive, with a really beautiful selection of produce (fish from Trouville, game, coffee beans) and prepared foods. The Eiffel Tower is in the background.

12th: Marché d'Aligre
(Every day, except Monday)
Nice affordable produce, in a quarter where the neighbouring shops wisely round out the selection.

16th: Marché du Président-Wilson
(Wednesday and Saturday)
Alongside the Musée d'Art Moderne, you'll find the star of market gardeners, Joël Thiébault. And you'll pay for it.

18th: Marché de Barbès
(Wednesday and Saturday)
You find everything here and it costs very little, including the most exotic produce. But the quality is not always up to par: choose carefully.

from the poulterer's hooks, like in a Flemish still life. On sunny days, with the smell of fresh basil in the air, you revive your link to the South of France stocking up on tomatoes and aromatic melons.

But the real pleasure of the market, what you savour most about it, is going there with your children. Going through the long list of things for them to learn about in the vendors' stands. Watching them become ecstatic over fish they've never seen before ("is that a shark, Papa?"); witnessing them being offered a bite of kofta or an olive; learning to recognize the different vegetables and fruit; and discovering tasty new words (apricot, sea-urchin, pheasant) and with them feeling the changing of seasons. It's an initiation to taste and the pleasure of food and fine produce. Pagan communion, sort of.

For the bucolic among you, the flower market on the Ile de la Cité (4th), is an explosion of colour and fragrance that will make your head spin. Open daily, except Sunday, when in its place there is an incredible bird market.

"Jean de Servigny was a small, svelte, rather bald and frail man. He was quite elegant, with a curly mustachio, clear eyes, and thin lips. He was one of these men of the night who seemed to have been born and raised on the boulevard; and who was tireless, though he always looked exhausted; vigorous though pale. He was a thin Parisian to whom the gymnasium, fencing, and the shower and steam rooms gave a nervous, artificial force. He was known for his parties as much as for his spirit, fortune and relations; for a kind of sociability, amiability and worldly gallantry that are particular to some men.

He was also a true Parisian. Careless, sceptical, changing, trainable, energetic and irresolute. He was capable of everything and nothing. Selfish on principle, with bursts of generosity, he was moderate about eating up his income, and his amusements were healthy. Indifferent and passionate, he was always letting himself go and was always taking himself in hand again, overcome by conflicting instincts and giving in to everything so that, when all was said and done, he could obey his idea of himself as a resourceful party boy, whose weathercock logic consisted in blowing with the wind and benefiting from circumstances, without ever taking the trouble to create them."

GUY DE MAUPASSANT
Yvette

BUYING A SHIRT

"His entire being, white cravat . . . jabot of shirt, ample brown redingote, the way he snuffed curving his arm, stirred up the kind of trouble produced when we see extraordinary men."
Gustave Flaubert

I don't know about you, but I never leave with the shirt I came to get. I wanted a simple white one in poplin, and the one I'm clutching as I make my way to the till is blue, with thin stripes. I often leave, of course, with more models than I wanted; the shirt shops are relentless traps.

The shirt is the man. It's the anchor of his wardrobe. His companion on a daily basis. You change shirts like you do ideas, and like ideas, you make sure they stay clean. And dignified. They may pretend to be virginal in the white of vespers or have that diva look with two-coloured cuffs; the might fall rigidly in the style of an Anglican pastor, or abandon themselves to the flowing curves of an Italian summer, they are never worn lightly. Shirts talk to us. So you might as well choose them with care.

Let's forget about tailoring for now, though tailored shirts have become more popular today (however you'll have to count on spending about €100). Rather, we'll navigate the dangerous coasts of ready-to-wear. Taste wreckers and profiteering merchants are always on the lookout for them. Buying a shirt is a perilous activity. Yet what a pleasure to find yourself at a good shirt maker's. So many shirts lie in wait, carefully folded on huge bookcases of dark wood, like so many volumes to skim through. Your eyes slide from model to model, jumping from solid to striped, herringbone to checked; and the range of colours is huge. Then there's the material you touch with your fingertips for a foretaste of the lavish softness on your bare skin (the height of luxury: when the cotton is silky, the shirt so fine you don't feel it, of Sea Island quality for example). Finally, there's the rundown on all the details: type and hold of the collar, removable collar stiffeners, gussets, stitching alignment, nacre buttons. All are pitiless revealers of quality.

You can already imagine how you're going to match them with just the right jacket and tie. That's it, you've made up your mind. You'll take this one, and that one. And that one . . .

TAILORED SHIRTS
(TO BE TRIED AT LEAST ONCE):

Swann et Oscar
1, rue de l'Arcade, 8th – 01 44 19 74 96

Samson
15, rue de Tournon, 6th – 01 43 25 13 60

JLR
45, avenue Paul-Doumer, 16th – 01 45 03 25 50

LUXURIOUS BESPOKE SHIRTS:

Didier Lucca
58, boulevard des Batignolles, 17th – 01 43 87 75 10

Édouard Courtot
113, rue de Rennes, 6th – 01 45 48 54 86

THE LITTLE NACRE ITEM:

This is an original gift idea for shirt lovers: nacre, tortoiseshell or silver collar stiffeners (be careful to choose lightweight ones), which are a good replacement for the standard moveable collar stiffeners. Luxury at an affordable price.

Thomas Pink
19, rue Francois-1er, 8th – 01 47 23 72 00

Maison Bonnet (écaille)
Passage des Deux-Pavillons,
5, rue des Petits-Champs, 1st – 01 42 96 46 35

YOU WON'T LOSE YOUR SHIRT ON THESE
READY-TO-WEAR SHIRT SHOPS:

Jo (Émile Lafaurie)
47, rue d'Orsel, 18th – 01 55 79 99 16

Melinda Gloss
42, rue de Saintonge, 3rd – 01 48 04 06 08

Kitsuné
52, rue de Richelieu, 1st – 01 42 60 34 28

Brooks Brothers
372, rue Saint-Honoré, 1st – 01 40 20 10 01

Breuer
14, rue de la Paix, 2nd – 01 42 60 68 31

Hackett
17, rue de Sèvres, 6th – 01 45 49 18 93

Alain Figaret
18/20, place de la Madeleine, 8th – 01 40 06 94 90

THE CREAM OF THE CROP:

Arnys
14, rue de Sèvres, 7th - 09 62 24 41 99

Charvet
28, place Vendôme, 1st – 01 42 60 30 70

HAVING BREAKFAST IN A LUXURY HOTEL

"A trip doesn't need a motive."
Nicolas Bouvier

Some days you'd like to escape from life. To free yourself from the hustle and bustle, and just leave. You want to enjoy the change of scenery a spontaneous trip affords, get away from it all. It can be said that luxury hotels were practically made for this. These long immobile steamships, moored to the quays of noisy avenues, await their passengers, offering their white silhouettes to them like landing piers.

One slips quietly into them in the morning, activating the revolving door as though passing a gate station, the forehead high, the eyes fixed on the distance. Generally, the restaurant dining room, of transatlantic dimensions, is empty of people at this unearthly hour. It yearns for a visit, a whisper, for tea and fresh-squeezed orange juice. It dreams of giving itself to the person who leaves his pastry crumbs behind.

Led by a person in uniform, you weave your way to your place, beautiful white table with a heavy cotton tablecloth; so this is where they store the sails. A warm breeze whistles in your ears, you sit back a bit in your chair, and you cast off your order. The music is low in the background. A "yes, but of course, Monsieur," concludes the order and you regain your solitude. You grab a book, often the same, the story of a trip or a worldly chronicle. You turn a few pages and, unless a buffet extends its Pantagruelian arms to you, your order arrives. You nibble sophisticated, familiar, sweet and salty things, like on vacation. The beauty of the place is a refuge. Everywhere you look, you rub your eyes.

And if fortune is smiling on you, there will be a soft foreign woman a few tables away, so that you can pretend to be lovers in a novel. A young girl on an extended holiday, whom you never dare approach before nightfall. But once night falls, you'll have already left.

DRIVING FAST IN THE BOIS DE BOULOGNE

"Even if you're in love like mad and in vain, you're less so at 200 km per hour."
Françoise Sagan

The best moment is very early in the morning. That's when the fleet of suburban cars no longer cause the Bois de Boulogne's avenues to glow with red lights. It's when you breathe in the smell of fresh grass, like picture postcard Normandy. The Bois de Boulogne is where you feel you're in the country in Paris. If the weather is at all good, you'll head over on the sly, for a little escapade, imitating the idle bourgeoisie of Françoise Sagan's novels, who would escape from Saint-Germain-des-Prés for an adulterous lunch under the trees.

You turned off the radio. You only want to hear the air, the wind and the engine. The pebbles that crunch at times under the tyres. The pleasure lies in the speed, which picks up little by little. You're driving on a country road, with soft curves followed by long straight lines, where the horsepower is pushed to the imposed limits. The heart speeds up also, the blood becomes excited, the eyes screw up over the landscape rolling by as you drive along it, becoming unreal with a continuous green and white band.

Even if you've been through it 100 times, you always get lost in the Bois de Boulogne, Parisians' civilized countryside, trodden for centuries. It's a tangle of horseback riders' alleys, sinuous roads, hidden refuges, skeet shooting, the Racing club, the vague rumour of the racetrack, with the Grande Cascade restaurant in your line of sight. You gently step on the gas, and it floods in, unleashing its mechanical storm. The car jumps ahead. You feel the speed slip into the wheels, which hug the asphalt in the white flow of early morning. The motor's beastly drone digs into the silence.

Yet the car does not perturb the languishing quietude of the ponds, called lakes here over a concern for grandeur. Taking a curve, it's the

remembrance of pleasant breakfasts at the Chalet des Îles that comes to mind (the simple joy of taking your beloved to the restaurant by ferry, like an aristocratic escape to Koblenz). The Bois de Boulogne condenses forgotten memories of outings in horse-drawn carriages into its greenery, memories of breathless lovers sitting in the back of saloon cars, of the presidential Citroën DS speedily weaving beneath the trees.

So you accelerate with determination, your nerves sharpening and provoking destiny until the next curve, the next stoplight. Driving fast in the Bois de Boulogne is the solitary pleasure of exceeding limits. Of dissolving time, reducing distances, mastering your machine, your reflexes, your life.

WHERE TO STOP TO GIVE YOUR MOTOR A REST

La Grande Cascade
allée de Longchamp, 16th – 01 45 27 33 51

Le Chalet des Îles
chemin de ceinture du lac Inférieur, 16th
01 42 88 04 69

L'Auberge du Bonheur
allée de Longchamp, 16th – 01 45 27 33 51

Bagatelle
42, route de Sèvres, 16th – 01 40 67 98 29

Le Tir aux Pigeons
route de l'Étoile, 16th – 01 40 67 95 44

NICOLAS BEDOS

Playwright, Drama Critic

NOON – MIDNIGHT

For a few years now, I've led a solitary life, until 6pm.
I spend my days in Paris reading and writing. So I only become
social, proper, hypocritical and elegant when the daylight starts
to fade.
Before that, I take a pair of not-quite pyjamas and an unkempt mop
of hair into my Marais neighbourhood. It's a place that's made me
happy, near a sensual and funny person who makes it even more
magical. I have lunch in silence in the Asian restaurants on the Rue
Volta and the Rue au Maire. For the past three years, the Paris I like
has been Chinese. I buy newspapers and magazines and I swallow
various types of rice, grilled ravioli and algae salads. All of that.
I drink iced tea as I skip through the news, the literary reviews
and the latest socialite gossip.
For example, I cook up Patrick Besson's column with a few
shrimp; Franz-Olivier Giesbert's column goes very well with
sate; and Frédéric Beigbeder's craziness is never as salty as when
accompanied with a green tea ice cream.
I read almost everything. The blather of the right and the inane
remarks of the left, meanness thought considered to be fine spirited,
praise you think is false.
Then I read *Le Monde* in a square on the Rue de Bretagne, and
then I "render it" back at my place, in the little moleskin notebooks
that all authors buy, certain the talent of Ernest Hemingway comes
with the price.
When night falls, I rediscover the high society of Paris, which I look
down on in daytime and which – at night – seems to wish us well.
The Paris of Saint-Germain, editors, producers, unfaithful women
and hip cocktail parties. And while giving a warm embrace to all
these, I yearn for the following noon, of long silent conversations
with the Korean waitress at the Chinese restaurant, who makes
fun of me and consequently, is attentive to what pleases me.

STUMBLING INTO A LATE-NIGHT BAR

"We're not used enough to casting a critical eye on the role of bar owners. These are people who have an actual place in keeping real civilization alive."
Aragon

It's the little night miracle. One in the morning, maybe later. You come out of an apartment, restaurant, a subsidized theatre or even the bed of a longstanding mistress. A few vapours of alcohol might even be making your head spin, unless it's the yakking of the crowd you've left or your lady's passionate kisses. So here you are on the street, slipping into the night air. Whether it's cold or not is not the question: you don't want to go home. You want a last drink. To continue the conversation (or finish it). To find a semblance of human warmth in the eyes of people you don't know.

You take a few random steps, have a few smokes, and a gust of wind ushers you into the first bar you see. It may be lit with yellowish neon, its Formica polished by 1950s lamps, or it might smell like beer and brandish a TV screen showing MTV; you don't notice very much. At this time of night, only one thing counts, and that's the few people clustered around the bar and bar owner with the friendly, scarlet face. You slip in noiselessly between the regulars, saying a good "bonsoir," and you order. Eyes meet. An old woman, two guys with the hands of a lumberjack and the neck of a bull, a frail little guy, dry as a stick, and a lost girl with very short hair. First, they say nothing (because of your tie?). Then once you take your first swallow, the conversation begins. The ice breaks over the glasses you drink. The drinks that in the wee hours bring people totally unlike one another together.

It's late at night, where everything blends together, where the most honest equality reigns. Where minds rather soaked in drink create friendships that are as fugitive as they are unlikely, but which are always sincere over an Armagnac.

To the right, the big guy with the air of an habitual criminal speaks with an incredibly soft voice; to the left, the short-haired girl allows an indolent snake to wind down her tattooed shoulders. Isn't it a generous hour, fleeting though it is? Winos and aristocrats, gays and straights, haves and have-nots fraternise, provided they have a heart and the nerve.

Besides, look, they've even forgotten your necktie.

A FEW BARS FOR A LATE-NIGHT TIPPLE:

Le Café Noir
65, rue Montmartre, 2nd
01 40 39 07 36

Le Sans Souci
65, rue Jean-Baptiste-
Pigalle, 9th
01 53 16 17 04

Au 36 Corneil
36, rue de Rochechouart,
9th

Le Béguin
2, rue du Cardinal-
Mercier, 9th
01 42 81 58 20

Swinging Londress
97, rue du Faubourg-
Saint-Denis, 10th
01 47 70 33 82

Le P'tit Bar
7, rue Richard-Lenoir, 11th

L'Alibi
11, rue Lapeyrère, 18th
01 42 52 23 50

Le Commerce
13, rue de Clignancourt,
18th – 01 46 06 25 63

Aux Folies
8, rue de Belleville, 20th
01 46 36 65 98

**And lots
of others . . .**

BUYING OLD-FASHIONED PASTRIES

*"Time swings in a censer
at the end of a brown string."*
Philippe Delerm

Now that pastries are becoming intellectual, at €5 a slice, the stars of all things sweet are structuring their cakes like Niemeyer's architectural constructions. Placing one of their "creations" in your mouth is a matter of acrobatics. And you'd like to do some good backpedalling. When the aces of ganache show their stuff in glossy women's magazines, and their new-look shops take inspiration from the coldness of jewellery stores, it's time to stake a claim for the sweet tooth. Because that's where the unique pleasure of pastry resides.

When you pick up a temptingly sweet pastry with your fingers, bite into it and feel the cream drip a bit along your lips, you can feel the Casanova-like sensuality of it. You throw yourself into it like a lover going to meet his beloved, the senses awakened, savouring the preliminaries and hoping, without really believing, that it will last a long time.

A few moments go by and that's it. It's gone, swallowed up. So yes, you want roundness there, where for now we are only being offered sharp angles.

So we start dreaming of opulence, of generous, happy cakes, with names that remind you of the countryside when Mass is over. Sundays full of Sunday things: éclairs, Paris-Brests, mille-feuilles, strawberry cakes, Saint-Honoré. Late 19th-century cakes: bulging, inconsistent, direct in their approach, with apparent simplicity but a sly springiness to them. They are not maliciously sweet, never leave you nauseated, and they offer their old-fashioned savours like a call to order.

Finally after all, eating a cake is to bite into memory. To once again find the tastes and colours of childhood in a polonaise with slightly soft meringue. And in a madeleine, of course.

TRADITIONAL PASTRY:

*Paris-Brest
and millefeuille:*
Carl Marletti
51, rue Censier, 5th

Baba and éclairs:
Pain de Sucre
14, rue Rambuteau, 3rd

*Cheesecake
and apple strudel:*
Stube
31, rue de Richelieu, 1st

Lemon meringue cake:
café Pouchkine
Printemps Mode
64, boulevard Haussmann, 8th

*Apple chausson
and millefeuille:*
Blé sucré
7, rue Antoine-Vollon, 12th

*Peach tart
and escargots:*
Du Pain et des Idées
34, rue Yves-Toudic, 10th

Scones:
Bread & Roses
7, rue de Fleurus, 6th

*Millefeuille and
seasonal fruit tarts:*
Stéphane Vandermeersch
278, avenue Daumesnil, 12th

Polish Brioche:
Kaffeehaus
11, rue Poncelet, 17th

Coffee éclairs and fraisier:
Carton
6, rue de Buci, 6th
et 150, avenue Victor-Hugo, 16th

SPORTING CUFFLINKS

"Beauty, my nice worry."
Valéry Larbaud

They show what kind of mood you're in. You don't take them out often, but when you do it's never by chance. Whether you've got a business meeting or an amorous one, a dressy evening or a crazy party, the occasions are out there, you just have to want to seize them. So you open the cigar box where you've placed them, finger the multicolour treasures inside in search of the pair that will go best with the circumstance. There is a pair for every nuance of character, every disposition: elegant (fine horse rider's bits), excessive (sparkling skulls), provocative (1960s-look naked woman), luxurious (mauve shagreen), gourmands (corkscrews). And if nothing grabs you, you'll turn to the small leather box containing the knot cufflinks, of an accidental roundness and in infinite variations, picking out the model that will subtly bring out your shirt colour and serve as a counterpoint to the shades of your necktie. You'll waste a few minutes more tapping them into the cuffs as big as sheets, ruminating over the word, savouring the very French, very Gascon feeling of being in d'Artagnan's shadow wearing "musketeer cuffs." You allow a sort of aristocracy of manners to fall over your attire. Which exceptionally, you have thought about, in advance savouring the looks people will give the ends of your sleeves.

Cufflinks are said to be an accessory, but they're essential. So in the future, have a look at the wrists of those you're talking to. Cufflinks mirror their soul.

IF YOU WANT TO PAY GOOD ATTENTION TO YOUR SHIRTSLEEVES:

Paul Smith (often funny, always colourful)
3, rue du Faubourg-Saint-Honoré, 8th – 01 42 68 27 10

Pinel & Pinel (delightfully original in shagreen or crocodile)
22, rue Royale, 8th
01 42 60 58 39

Dunhill (bulldog heads, very British)
15, rue de la Paix, 2nd
01 42 61 57 58

Tiffany (Barbell, timeless)
6, rue de la Paix, 2nd
01 40 20 20 20

Charvet (knot cufflinks, Charvet luxury for next to nothing)
28, place Vendôme, 1st
01 42 60 30 70

Milus (very chic oscillating movement of a Swiss watch)
Sold at makers of jewellery watches.

THE LITTLE LUXURY ITEM I INDULGE IN:

Samuel Gassmann hand makes, in his atelier, one-of-a-kind cufflinks (often from antiques dealers). Limited series or original ceremonial models. Wonderfully offbeat and elegant. From €90 to €300.
Sold at Eglé Bespoke - 26 rue du Mont Thabor, 1st - 01 44 15 98 31 - samuelgassmann.com

CYCLING

"Cycling is a show of elegance."
Louis-Ferdinand Céline

You have to be a little crazy to cycle in Paris. You have to have a derailleur's kamikaze nature, be a handlebar nut. So think about it: terrifying traffic, hoards of pedestrians ignorant of stoplights, foolhardy bikers racing along in the cycling paths, unpredictable weather: you need to be terribly unaware of these things to hop on a bicycle of a morning. But you have to say cycling in Paris is a rarely found joy.

Of course, you have to choose your moment. Off-peak hours, a Saturday or Sunday morning before croissant time, a long weekend in May, a holiday, a general strike day, off-peak hours in Paris in summer: in the end, the occasions are numerous. So you get your bike from your cellar, hallway or balcony, the little bijou you've pampered for so long. It's got everything: an old frame with elegant articulations (nothing to do with the clunky handlebars of modern hybrid bikes), two purses on the carrier, which for once is deserving of its name, chrome mirrors, a flat leather seat, tanned as the skin of an old Corsican.

You get on, start to pedal and off you go. Straight away, the silence is striking. If you're bicycle is well adjusted, it's like clockwork without the ticking. There's no noise, not even a clicking of the chain, not a rubbing of tire against the fender; it starts to move with a whisper of air against our cheeks. Looking all around, you are part of the landscape, capturing the sensations of your body, where every part is contributing. Wandering through Paris on your bicycle is to be Paris. To physically sense the smells, views, reliefs, plateaus and sudden hills, to be rocked in a cradle of total liberty. It's an engine that needs nothing to continue moving ahead, if only a bit of muscle and enthusiasm, a little queen that's been with us since childhood.

So, if by chance you come across a cobblestoned square, near the huge clusters of trees along the Avenue de Breteuil, you suddenly turn into a little boy again, the one who wore out the tyres of a little poppy-red tricycle (was this gift from his parents a jockey model?) on the side paths nearby. With every spin of a wheel comes a new memory.

ON BICYCLES:

Urban Solutions
13, rue du 4-Septembre, 2nd
01 42 86 84 03

Bicloune
93, boulevard Beaumarchais, 3rd
01 42 77 58 06

Au Point Vélo Hollandais
81-83, boulevard Saint-Michel, 5th
01 43 54 85 36

Cycle Centre
30, rue Grégoire-de-Tours, 6th
01 43 29 09 04

Vélo Vintage
58, rue du Ruisseau, 18th
06 13 13 42 27 (Eddy)
ou 06 03 89 61 21 (Hugo)

And:
Ecox
(specialising
in electric bicycles)
23, rue de Rivoli, 4th
01 42 71 56 39

DAVID
FOENKINOS
Writer

THE SWITZERLAND OF PARIS

For more than 10 years I lived opposite the Bibliothèque Nationale de France, or the François Mitterrand library as Parisians call it. This is why people take me for a psychopath of real estate. Especially in the beginning, when the neighbourhood was only a foetus: my building was the only one to keep company with the library. From my balcony, I can contemplate it. And I watch it every evening with the same emotion. It's an antidote to lassitude. In summer, what I love to do is walk along the esplanade. In the evening there's no one left there. It's so quiet. It's the Switzerland of Paris.

AN ITINERARY FOR LOVERS

A love life is summed up in this sentence from Sacha Guitry:
"We want one another, we embrace; then boredom sets in,
and for attacks of self-anger we brace."
Here's a little illustration of it in a bittersweet itinerary,
made in Paris.

1. WHERE TO MEET HER

All of Paris is a storehouse
of attractive women. If you're afraid
of the open sky, wait for nightfall
and run to the cellar.

Le Pompon
39, rue des Petites-Écuries, 10th
01 53 34 60 85

2. WHERE TO HAVE LUNCH
TO GET TO KNOW ONE ANOTHER

She's a woman. You hope a bit light.
What she eats, too.

KGB
25, rue des Grands-Augustins, 6th
01 46 33 00 85

3. WHERE TO TAKE HER
FOR THAT FIRST DRINK

For a vital late afternoon,
be chic but not showy,
in a place that's not well known.

Le Bar 30
15, rue Boissy-d'Anglas, 8th
01 44 94 14 27

4. WHERE TO TAKE HER FOR
DINNER FOR THE FIRST TIME

What could be better than
a theatrical setting and candles
to kick things off?

Pétrelle
34, rue Pétrelle, 9th – 01 42 82 11 02

5. WHERE TO FINALLY KISS HER

Strong alcohol, soft music,
deep banquettes and dim lighting:
the cocktails have already proven
themselves.

Park Hyatt Vendôme
5, rue de la Paix, 2nd – 01 58 71 12 34

6. WHERE TO TAKE HER FOR THAT LAST DRINK

Though you may prefer her boudoir,
this one isn't bad, either.

Curio Parlor
16, rue des Bernardins, 5th
01 44 07 12 47

7. WHERE TO CINCH THE DEAL

Because hotels are a journey.
Even in Paris. And you want it to be
unforgettable and sensual.

Hôtel Amour
8, rue de Navarin, 9th – 01 48 78 31 80

8. WHERE TO ASK FOR HER HAND

Luxurious and intimate, but not
overly so. Sumptuous meals,
but not overly so.

La Table du Lancaster
7, rue de Berri, 8th – 01 40 76 40 18

9. ONE YEAR LATER . . .

To surprise her and give a little
polish to the humdrum life
you share (be bold and book
a private room).

Lapérouse
51, quai des Grands-Augustins, 6th
01 43 26 68 04

10. AND TO BREAK UP

There's only one rule to memorize:
crowds neutralize shouting (but not
tears). So go to the very, very busy
brasserie with the fated name.

Terminus Nord
23, rue de Dunkerque, 10th – 01 42 85 05 15

CHOOSING WINE

"Wine is like a man: you'll never know how much esteem you hold for it, or how much disdain, how much love for it or how much hate, nor of how many sublime actions or monstrous deeds it is capable."

Charles Baudelaire

Ah, that little question before you dine. Choosing a wine in a restaurant is going back to school, solving a problem on the board, in front of the entire class, a rotten equation. And you haven't always done your homework.

Yet all the pleasure lies in setting out the parameters (everyone's preferences, the dishes ordered, how the meal will unfold), mixing up what's left of your knowledge and memory and asking, after that last assent from the group, with a victorious finger pointing to a line on the menu, when the sommelier leans over your shoulder. Obviously it's easier when you're one-on-one than in a big group, as there are fewer variables. Then comes the bottle. You await the first sip, the satisfied smile, the glass reposing in peace. But rest assured, there's not much risk to this game, as the guilty indulgence of your friends spare you from acid comments when the tasting begins. Only the silence or a compliment whispered will indicate if you've failed miserably. That can happen.

At the wine store, it's something else. You show your notebook of grievances, detail the circumstances, who the wine is for and why, whether it's for a gift, a dinner, an aperitif. Once the stage is set, you'll get the pleasure of hearing yourself state your wishes, words that flow like a little prose poem, a haiku from the bottle: "A rather strong red with body and power, a bit velvety." Or, "A fresh, crispy white, rather dry but bitter, you see?" Naturally, if you have chosen your wine merchant well, he sees. Your second layer of happiness comes in choosing the bottle from among the two or three suggested to you. Purists don't drink the labels; aesthetes never buy an ugly bottle. That's how it goes; nestled everywhere, beauty guides them, even in a table wine. Follow their example. Go for the bottle and intoxication.

IN WINE LIES HAPPINESS:

Versant Vins
33 bis, rue Charlot, 3rd – 01 42 72 34 85

A young woman from the Loire Valley, Jeanne Galinié, sells bottles that are often natural, but not dogmatic. Beautiful shop in the heart of the Marché des Enfants-Rouges. And you can open them at the restaurant next door.

Chapitre 20
8, rue Saint-Paul, 4th – 01 77 15 20 72

Emmanuel Dupuis had the bright idea of opening a wine shop specialized in whites. Excellent French selection, but there is also wine from Germany, Austria and Spain. It is also the only bookstore in Paris specialized in books about wine.

Le Vin en Tête
48, rue Notre-Dame-de-Lorette, 9th – 01 53 21 90 17

A super selection of very natural wines but not only, by an enthusiastic team (one of the founders, Christophe Beau, is now a winegrower). A bonus: it has an excellent wine bar: goodness.

La Cave des Papilles
35, rue Daguerre, 14th – 01 43 20 05 74

The reference when it comes to organic and natural wine. A fine, smart selection of the best of today's winegrowers. It never becomes fundamentalist.

Les Crus du Soleil
146, rue du Château, 14th – 01 45 39 78 99

This is the wine shop that allowed us to discover Languedoc-Roussillon wine in Paris. The selection is perfect: all the pioneers are here, as are the second, third and fourth waves.

Des Mets et des Vins
15, rue d'Auteuil, 16th – 01 45 20 68 07

A band of jolly fellows, stowaways from the business world, recommend food and wine pairings: all the bottles are fabulous finds from French vineyards. They are set out on the shelves by types of meal and price.

MORE TRADITIONAL
BUT TRULY COMPETENT:

Legrand Filles et Fils
1, rue de la Banque, 2nd – 01 42 60 07 12

Cave Bossetti
34, rue des Archives, 4th – 01 48 04 07 77

Les Caprices de l'Instant
12, rue Jacques-Cœur, 4th – 01 40 27 89 00

Caves Augé
116, boulevard Haussmann, 8th – 01 45 22 16 97

Du Vin et des Bulles (from Champagne)
6, rue Blanche, 9th – 01 48 74 41 85

Rouge, Blanc et Bulles
12, rue Parrot, 12th – 01 43 47 45 14

If you read only one book about finding the good little wines that should make up your cellar, make it this one.
Superb finds, picked up far from the well-worn paths of the straight-laced sommelier world, and a real feast of reading.

Le Petit Lapaque des vins de copains
Sébastien Lapaque
Actes Sud

LOOKING IN WINDOWS

"Some lights in the windows of big buildings."
Patrick Modiano

When winter nights become opaque, Paris turns to balconies.

In summer it's not the same. Life happens outside, its little plays unfold on café terraces, the order of the day changing with the flexible hours spent at the parks and gardens. Everything is to discover, with no surprise and no mystery. But when it's October – and sometimes even earlier – pushed by the cold and the dying light, the actors move, fold up the set: the play happens indoors, prodded by cold air and dying light.

The street performances are pretty interesting. Thousands of windows light up as soon as the afternoon is over. Thousands of dormers display either banal or extraordinary scenes to the passerby, scenes of a reclusive life. How can you not look? Your eye is attracted by high golden ceilings, a chandelier glowing in the middle of a room, a huge painting or a sleeping cookshelf. Then figures move around. You can glimpse them slipping from one room to another, becoming absorbed for a second in an obscure task, pensively smoking a cigarette at the balcony, window half open.

Every apartment is a theatre where lives are played out. The play starts at 6pm. You look in the windows, imagining tragic or grandiose destinies, flamboyant or dull people, a multitude of destinies unfolding with the toss of dice, and so many lives moulded by habit and monastically regulated. Behind the windowpanes are secrets and yearnings, cries, love lives torn apart, time passing, thwarted ambitions and hopes for better tomorrows. It's enough to get your imagination going, weaving the threads of a Parisian story.

Looking inside apartments is to live in a pastoral novel.
It's a Patrick Modiano life, observing.

WHERE TO SET YOUR STAGE

The big quiet apartments of the south edge of the 16th arrondissement, the aristocratic buildings of the 7th, the buildings with small-paned windows in the Marais, the little houses in the Cité des Fleurs in the 13th, the Grand Siècle luxury at the huge windows of the Ile Saint-Louis, the chic discretion of the big buildings hidden behind the trees around the Champ-de-Mars, and the Quai d'Orsay: there is no lack of apartment settings in Paris. You just need to follow the footlights.

BEST
OF
BURGERS

"The Americans must be helped."
Pierre-Augustin Caron de Beaumarchais

What a shameful pleasure. At a time when meals are light as feathers, when vegetables are at the pinnacle of success and organics are on every street corner, feasting on a hamburger has become an act of resistance, a way of being healthily anti-conformist.

We must say the burger has lots of things against it: American, it packs loads of calories and lies back in a far corner of teenage memory. Hamburgers are sacrilegious. So why keep yourself from eating them? Especially since you can find them easily at respectable Paris eateries. The hamburger is a bit like the Porthus of food musketeers. It's not that sophisticated, but it's a good chap; valiant; its power and portliness make it a pleasant companion and one you can count on. Avoid the sloppy one, however; make sure it holds together a bit: the homemade bun has to be soft, the loosely ground meat has to be thick and juicy, and the veggies have to be fresh and crunchy (lettuce, onions tomato, pickles), the ketchup a bit sweet, but not syrupy. And don't shrink from the proper side order. Salad and a hamburger? Nope, never heard of it. Get it with the homemade fries, a historical counterpoint and absolute must for this sinful pleasure. Again, the fries must be of excellent extraction, crispy and soft, served so hot you can burn your fingers on them. Just a tad shiny. For the rest, you can eat the burger with your two hands or politely cut it with your fork and knife. Either is allowed, as long as you take big bites. Finally you need a straightforward red to drink with it. A Ventoux or Côtes de Castillon will give it that Franco-American air that Jean Seberg would not have denied. It's like going back to the Saint-Germain clubs, when "American" was synonymous in Paris with jazz and cigarettes. Hurry up buddies, this burger's for you!

AMERICAN STYLE:

H.A.N.D.
39, rue de Richelieu, 1st – 01 40 15 03 27

Breakfast in America
17, rue des Écoles, 5th – 01 43 54 50 28

Blend Hamburger
44, rue d'Argout, 2nd – 01 40 26 84 57

PDG
8, rue de Ponthieu, 8th – 01 42 56 19 10

Floor's
100, rue Myrha, 18th – 01 42 62 08 08

FRENCH STYLE:

Le Dalí
(hôtel Meurice)
228, rue de Rivoli, 1st – 01 44 58 10 10
(Designated best hamburger in the world
by the *New York Times*, and the most authentically
luxurious one at a whopping €36.)

Glou
101, rue Vieille-du-Temple, 3rd – 01 42 74 44 32

Maison de l'Aubrac
37, rue Marbeuf, 8th – 01 43 59 05 14

DAVID
ABIKER
Writer, Journalist

I SOAK UP THE EVENING

I've always had this fear of "addresses," good spots, trendy bars and restaurants. Doubtless it's the panicky fear of not being where I belong, of not being expected and not being enough like the clientele. It's the anxiety of not being of them, before even being there. I can't help it. A restaurant or bistro is a place you don't look for, that you don't reference. It can't be found on a map or on the Internet. To feel good somewhere, I just need to go through the door and soak up the habit. I'm starting to be like an old cat. For me, "Comme d'habitude" should never have been a sad song. Habits are what dress a man, what gives a shine to his leather; they are "your own addresses," choices as happy as the mistakes you are stubborn about repeating for better and sometimes for worse. So here is where I like to go in Paris. I like to go to Carette for a coffee, to read the papers and ask myself where the chic, Mediterranean patrons get their breasts, these women in such a hurry with their long fingernails and Amazon-like boots. I like to eat at André, near Europe 1, where the waitresses wear a white apron over their black skirts. They ask me what I'm reading and serve me with the retro zeal of subservient, complicit workers. I also like Chaumette, near the Maison de la Radio. Chaumette's dining room feels like a country house, feels like it's for gourmand senior citizens. If I were not who I am, I would have been an old dandy or a tea-sipping Englishwoman, which is why I also go to Deux-Abeilles, a tearoom with pastries and Toile de Jouy fabric, which reminds me of the family homes I never had. These are my habitual places, and it's precisely because they're a little outmoded and are where I live in my way, that they've become small pleasures.
I leave the lounge bars and their airport style compilations to young people. To them as well I leave the nice bars at the Bastille and their youthful, cosmopolitan brouhaha; and the entire hospitality/restaurant sector with its stars, wine cellars and palaver. Habits, a memory and a hint of melancholy will never put me in the avant-garde of places where you have to be. I'm only a man, I'm not a tour guide. You won't change my plate or round napkin. At night, I soak things up.

COMING BACK FROM THE COUNTRY

"The rainfall came through very quickly, now there's a lull. The fields are steaming on either side of the road. . . . At 150 km per hour, I am crossing layers of reminiscences."

Paul Guimard

The highway flies past. The approaching golden red light of evening floods the fields here in the Beauce region. The weekend is over. We've closed the house, the shutters, the door, the garden gates. We've stuffed ourselves into the car, heading to Paris, and we don't want to think too much about the traffic jams already awaiting us about an hour from here.

We'd have stayed longer. The air was so soft. The evening was falling slowly over the garden, finally becoming peaceful, stretching out its arms to us. It was again the quiet hour, the hour of pale, shining light, when last songs of the birds could be heard. The smell of the lawn, wet from the last sprinkling, followed us to the car.

Now it's 8pm. The radio fills the interior with peaceful music. The weather is warm. A woman's voice, warm and Slavic, peels off the names of the pieces. You'd like to note them, remember the adagio of Mozart's Piano Concerto No. 23 and buy it on Monday. But with your hands on the wheel and your mind a bit elsewhere, it never happens.

Like every weekend, time went far too quickly. You give the rundown and what you didn't do: repair the old chair in the hallway, choose the paint that you'll use for the upstairs bedroom, plant that blue hydrangea that's been sitting in its pot for two weeks, read the newspapers you brought on purpose from Paris to take the time to look at them outside in the garden, visit the neighbours and taste the Sauvignon they'd brought just for you.

In the car, Sunday is not quite finished and the week ahead not yet really

started, but you're already noting the commitments and dinners for the coming days, like so many reassuring road markers, warm references that punctuate time until the next weekend. Paris is calling us back to its anarchical, worldly lifestyle.

Then there is silence. The car, whose headlights are now lit, slips into the dusk. You hope you haven't left anything in the house, but in any case it's not that big a deal, you'll be back there in a week.

WANT A FEW MORE IDEAS?

The things to be enjoyed all day in Paris are countless, and here are a few tidbits.

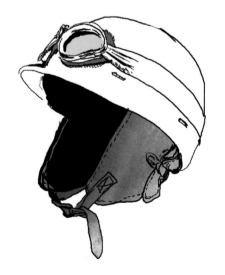

Have you heard of Chapal? It's that quiet little French brand that gentlemen drivers like so much, which won theheart of New Yorkers in the 1920s. In their Paris showroom, you can find all the vintage accessories for the man in a hurry that were so dear to Paul Morand. Gloves, leather jackets, biker's goggles, helmets and soft leather headbands, without which you can hardly imagine rolling along in a roadster.

Chapal
244, rue de Rivoli, 1st
06 16 11 56 60 (by appointment)

Paris is brimming with specialized bookstores, attracting aficionados of photography, graphic novels and garter belts. The Monte-en-l'Air offers a very specialized selection – necessarily piquant – and it's not at all politically correct: the history of anarchism, gangsters, suicide, and duels. Bad boy things, in fact.

Le Monte-en-l'Air
71, rue de Ménilmontant, 20th – 01 40 33 04 54

Rue Clerc has since 1936 housed an Italian grocer of the first order, owned from the beginning by the same family from Parma. The decor hasn't changed an iota, and the Italian cold cuts are to die for. There's also a wonderful cheese assortment. You won't leave without having slipped a few divine slices of Mortadella into your shopping bag. It's as fine and light as pink lace, and you can grease up your fingers eating it.

Davoli
36, rue Cler, 7th – 01 45 51 23 41

If your pots, pans and mixing bowls no longer meet up to your culinary ambitions, there's only one solution: put down your apron and run over to Dehillerin near Les Halles and to La Bovida. Get lost in their treasure troves of professional cooking utensils. You'll find everything you need to be a great chef.

La Bovida
36, rue Montmartre, 1st – 01 42 36 09 99

Dehillerin
18, rue Coquillière, 1st – 01 42 36 53 13

What a pleasure to wear a beautiful pair of gloves, in summer and winter both. It is even said that some aesthetes slip them on to read the newspaper, to keep the ink stains off. Aside from the elegant and renowned Maison Fabre at the Palais Royal, you can also find superb models in the most diverse materials at Hélion Gantier (since 1925). While you're at it, you can get some very chic, woven, openwork driving gloves. The ideal gift.

Hélion Gantier
22, rue Tronchet, 8th – 01 47 42 26 79

With organics so highly popular in Paris, you look for good places to buy quality produce at reasonable prices. The most discreet, that really tries not to stick out, is called Maison POS. The aromas of old-time market gardeners can be found there along with a creamery of character. And you won't have to take out your gold card when you go to the cash register. The produce seems to have been harvested the day before, and the boss is a bit of a misanthrope, which has a kind of charm.

Maison POS
90, rue de Charonne, 11th

For next to nothing at Doursoux, a surplus store in the shadow of Montparnasse, you'll find army jackets that never go out of style and are great for weekends. There's the safari jacket in airflex cotton, for example, a made-in-France copy of the jacket worn by the British army during its campaign in Palestine in 1917 then in Burma between 1942 and 1945.

Doursoux
3, passage Alexandre, 15th – 01 43 27 00 97

When the idea of having a cane or an umbrella becomes titillating (how great you'll look going down the Grands Boulevards, twirling your umbrella with each step you take under the leaden sky), don't think twice: go straight to Antoine, doubtless one of the oldest specialty shops in Paris, since 1745.

Antoine
10 avenue de l'Opéra, 1st – 01 42 96 01 80

When you want to withdraw:
Alexandra Sojfer
218, boulevard Saint-Germain, 7th – 01 42 22 17 02

The 19th-century arcades of the Palais-Royal have since 1862 sheltered one of the most surprising spots in Paris, a curiosity shop entirely devoted to pipe smoking. It is run by Rakel Van Kote, a colourful, wordy person.
Of course you can buy a few models and have your own pipe repaired. The rumour is that the Conseil Constitutionnel very nearby likes to meet there.

A l'Oriental
19/21, galerie de Chartres, Palais-Royal, 1st – 01 42 96 43 16

On a Sunday morning, you can go back in time by winding your way through the alleys of the Marché aux Puces de Saint-Ouen, the flea market. The era you choose is entirely up to you. For us, because it's a vintage thing, it would be the 1950s and '60s, with a little bit of orange plastic overlap into the '70s. The stands are fun, filled with the familiarly shaped furniture anchored in our childhood memories. Head down the Rue des Rosiers beyond the Marché Paul Bert to take the very last alley to the left, behind the gate . . .

Marché Paul Bert
Allée du Design
Impasse Simon, 93400 Saint-Ouen

Though their evening parties are less of a secret today than in the beginning, Les Ambassadeurs has the knack for organising (too rarely unfortunately) improbable costume balls, blending glamour with an adolescent spirit. Find yourself in the 1930s, in Marie-Antoinette's court or fully in the 19th century: these people dare to do anything. And they do it with derision, champagne and good humour, never departing from their friendly, slightly sophisticated style. In short, at Les Ambassadeurs they don't say "my darling" after every sentence.

www.lesambassadeurs.org

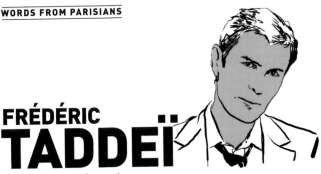

FRÉDÉRIC
TADDEÏ

Journalist, Columnist

NEVER READ GUIDEBOOKS

Another guidebook asking me for addresses and advice. Supposedly elegant addresses and advice.

Paris for Men, it's called and for once, I really want to answer.

If things as exciting and complex as "Paris" and "elegance" can be reduced to a few addresses you get from a guidebook, they would be irritated by the veneration they elicit. The secret of elegance is that there's no secret. As for Paris, it's a city, that's all. It shouldn't be taken too seriously. I only know one rule: never read guidebooks. There are too many amateurs. Too many professionals. Too many pigeons. You could almost use a guidebook in a place where you only stay a few days, to deal with the most important things first. But not in the city you live in. It would be a little like trying to get information about the woman of your life from her exes. Not very elegant. Believe me, the guidebook for this or that is the Paris of other people. It will never be yours. Ignore the "good addresses" in *Paris for Men*, they're everyone's addresses. Instead, invent a Paris that's just for you. The elegant thing is to be unique.

One man's neckties do no make another man happy. Take the famous Suite Impériale of the Ritz, with its six-meter-high ceilings. You think that suits everybody? Carnegie, who wasn't very tall, felt tiny inside it.

He preferred to move into the smallest room in the hotel, much better suited to his size. That was elegant. And to be elegant, all methods are good. The best would be to forget the advice you've received. Including this advice.

When the two gravediggers had thrown a few shovelfuls of earth onto the coffin to cover it, they again got up, and one of them, addressing Rastignac, asked him for their pourboire. Eugène dug into his pocket and found nothing there. He was forced to borrow a franc from Christophe. This event, so meaningless a thing in itself, gave Rastignac a terrible feeling of sadness. Night fell; the humid twilight set him on edge; he looked at the tomb and in it buried his last youthful tear. It was a tear torn by divine emotion from a pure heart, and it splashed into the sky from the earth where it fell. He crossed his arms and contemplated the clouds. Seeing him thus, Christophe left him.

Rastignac, now alone, took a few steps toward the high point of the cemetery and saw Paris winding flat along the two banks of the Seine, where lights were beginning to shine. His eyes remained almost avidly fixed between the column of the Place Vendôme and the Dôme des Invalides, where the polite society he wanted to be a part of lived. The look he tossed over this hive of activity seemed to draw out its honey ahead of time, and he uttered these grandiose words: "It's between the two of us now!"

HONORÉ DE BALZAC
Le Père Goriot

CONTENTS

PRAISE, PLEASE!

To Anne-Laure, my Parisian.
To Étienne, Thomas and Hippolyte, little Right and Left Bank Parisians.
To Gabrielle, who follows in their footsteps sashaying.

It is said that writing is a solitary exercise. Perhaps. But not always. Take this book for example. You can't imagine everyone I'd like to thank for their help, from the most modest to the most decisive help. It is because of them that today, you're holding this item in your hands. So with the risk I am taking on of possibly forgetting someone (may that person forgive me), I'm taking this opportunity to call them onto the stage with me.

Thanks to Fany Péchiodat, with whom, as we shared a jar of rillette and a glass of white wine, the idea for this book came about.

Thanks to Volcy Loustau and Fabienne Kriegel of Éditions du Chêne for trusting in me and opening the doors of their beautiful house to me.

Thanks to Juliette Ranck and Léopold Charniot, my artistic alger egos, for their immense talent and infinite patience. Without them this book would lack savour. It was a great joy to work with them.

Thanks to Mateo Baronnet, our graphics team leader, who wasn't afraid when we spoke of the *New Yorker* and who did such a great job of putting our texts and illustrations to music.

Always on the lookout for the best addresses, they are my eyes, ears, sometimes my mouth, my clues, my friends. I thank them here for all they have done: Frédéric Adida, Xavier Barbe, Charles Barraine, Cyril Boissy, Frédéric Brun, Nicolas Castro, Julien Despinasse, Emery Doligé, Arnaud Duhem, Julien Fouin, Alexis Fraikin, Egmont Labadie, Olivier Magny, Nicolas Nowak, Jean-Bernard Nussbaumer, Oscar, François Pourcher, Geoffroy Ropert, Nicolas Sauzay, Marc Simon, Guillaume Tesson, Gabriel Vachette, Pierre Vallet, Bruno Verjus.
And as for women (we need them), Claire, Clarisse, Emmanuelle, Isabelle and Roxane.
Thanks to François Simon and Emmanuel Rubin. They gave me the irrepressible desire to dip my pen into the *sauce gribiche* to write about peas. They remain my masters on the subject.
Thanks to David Abiker, Franck Baranger, Nicolas Bedos, Frédéric Beigbeder, Charles Dantzig, David Foenkinos, Francis Kurkdjian, Patrick Roger and Frédéric Taddeï for having believed in this crazy idea and for having shared, with such talent, the things they enjoy about Paris.

Thanks to the Gros Mecs for being here, not often and sometimes tardily.
Thanks to Guillaume Gallienne of La Comédie-Française for his elegance and encouragements.
Thanks to God, Mom and Dad for making me a man, and to Mankind for having created all these admirable things.
Thanks to the die-hard readers who read till the last line of these thanks. You are heros.

"In rust we trust"

EDITOR: **VOLCY LOUSTAU**
GRAPHICS: **LOT49** | **MATEO BARONNET**
TRANSLATION: **JEANNE CHEYNEL**
COORDINATION FOR THE ENGLISH EDITION AND PAGE LAYOUT: **ELSE**
PRODUCTION: **MARION LANCE**

PRINTED IN SPAIN BY ESTELLA GRAFICAS
REGISTRATION OF COPYRIGHT: AVRIL 2012
978-2-81230-582-5
34/8474/8